Break the Bipolar Cycle

A DAY-BY-DAY GUIDE TO

LIVING WITH

BIPOLAR DISORDER

Elizabeth Brondolo, Ph.D., and Xavier Amador, Ph.D.

New York   Chicago   San Francisco   Lisbon   London   Madrid   Mexico City
Milan   New Delhi   San Juan   Seoul   Singapore   Sydney   Toronto

Library of Congress Cataloging-in-Publication Data

Brondolo, Elizabeth.
    Break the bipolar cycle : a day-by-day guide to living with bipolar disorder / by Elizabeth Brondolo and Xavier Amador.
        p.   cm.
    Includes bibliographical references and index.
    ISBN 0-07-148153-2
    1. Manic-depressive illness—Popular works.   I. Amador, Xavier Francisco.
II. Title.

RC516.B77   2008
616.89′5—dc22   2007026658

3 4 5 6 7 8 9 10 11 12 13 14 15 16 17 18 19 20 21 22   FGR/FGR   0 9 8

ISBN 978-0-07-148153-3
MHID   0-07-148153-2

Interior design by Susan H. Hartman

McGraw-Hill books are available at special quantity discounts to use as premiums and sales promotions or for use in corporate training programs. To contact a representative, please visit the Contact Us pages at www.mhprofessional.com.

Since the case illustrations in this book are taken from Dr. Brondolo's clinical and consultation practices, these examples are written in the singular first person to reflect Dr. Brondolo's professional activities. The names of the patients and some details of their activities have been altered to respect confidentiality.

This book is printed on acid-free paper.

To my family, Tom, Emma, and Elena Brondolo, with love

—E.B.

To my patients and friends with bipolar disorders

—X.A.

Contents

Conclusion

Preface

Bipolar spectrum disorders (BSDs) are a group of disorders all of which involve cycling moods. But BSDs are also accompanied by a wide range of other symptoms that affect not just your mood but also your energy, your memory and thinking, and your connection with other people. Because the symptoms change or cycle, it may feel like you are always losing ground, never gaining control over your life.

But it doesn't have to be that way. A systematic approach to understanding and managing BSD can make the cycles more predictable and more controllable. We wrote this book to help you break the bipolar cycle—to get some momentum on recovery.

The Big Picture

Bipolar spectrum disorders are finally getting the attention they deserve. The media is covering the story, so the public is more aware of BSDs. Researchers have a clearer understanding of how many people are affected (about 3 to 8 percent of the U.S. population). They have been able to document the personal and financial costs to those with the condition and to their families, friends, and employers.

This new understanding about BSDs changes public policy. Many more research dollars are being spent than ever before, and the science is improving. New medicines and psychotherapies have been—and continue to be—developed. Many people are treated effectively with medicines and psychotherapy. And with more and more celebrities sharing stories of their own struggles with BSD, the stigma has been greatly reduced. So things will get even better.

Here's the part that's a little more difficult. BSD is a harder, more painful, and more disabling disorder than doctors previously recognized. Of course, if you have BSD, you may already know this. But your family, friends, or employers might not. It is not unusual for our BSD patients to tell us that people get angry at them for not "getting better." At different points, you may have wondered if you're not getting better because you are just lazy or difficult. But in fact, it's the BSD that is difficult.

Why Is It So Difficult?

BSD is difficult because it involves problems in two key areas: *mood regulation* and *information processing*. You know you experience problems with the quality, stability, and intensity of your mood and your energy level. But the mood symptoms are not the only problem. BSD can also be accompanied by impairments in information processing—in your ability to pay attention, to remember, and to organize information. Combined, these mood-regulation and information-processing problems affect your motivation and functioning—your ability to start the process of recovery, to accomplish your personal and professional goals, and to develop meaningful relationships with other people.

BSD is difficult because it is a stress-related disorder. Stress increases your symptoms, and your symptoms make it harder to tolerate stress. Even little events that might not have caused a moment's worry before you got sick can now create substantial stress. To recover, you need to recognize and manage stress effectively.

And BSD is difficult because it is a cycling disorder. Just when you think you have a handle on your symptoms, the situation changes. This can leave you and your loved ones feeling discouraged and defeated.

But you can gain control. In *Break the Bipolar Cycle*, we give you the scientific and practical information you need to manage this disorder more effectively day-to-day.

The Bottom Line

Bipolar spectrum disorders are neurobiological disorders that affect you on multiple levels. The psychiatrists have good options for you, but the medications aren't perfect, and they don't do the whole job. *You* can do a lot to optimize your treatment and enhance your recovery.

The key to recovery is achieving a stable mood. Stability doesn't mean you never have highs or lows. It means your moods make sense—they are in sync with what is happening in your life. You have some confidence that you can tolerate a little stress, and when you get upset (or excited) about something, you can regain your balance reasonably quickly. As you achieve sustained mood stability, you will see improvement in your motivation and your accomplishments. Maybe not rapidly but steadily.

You can optimize your ability to achieve sustained mood stability by working closely with your treatment providers and your support network. Together with your treatment team you will monitor your symptoms and adjust your treatment to help you achieve a stable mood.

The goal of *Break the Bipolar Cycle* is to give you the expertise you need to rapidly recognize symptoms and stressors. This information can help you and your treatment team decide if you need a course correction in your medications, therapy, or activities to keep your mood stable. With experience and careful monitoring, you will learn which treatments help you control your symptoms most effectively—and with the fewest possible side effects.

As you succeed in controlling your symptoms, BSD will become much more manageable and much less scary. Most important, as your BSD gets under better control, it will stop being the primary focus of your attention. You will be able to move ahead and concentrate on other things that matter.

We encourage you to be proactive, systematic, persistent, and collaborative in your approach to recovery. So although we use the term *patient* in this book, we recognize that this illness affects *people*. We strongly believe that proactive consumers who are educated and involved in the management of their treatment have the best chance at recovery. In our experience the more systematic your approach to recovery, the more likely it is that you will reach your goals.

We hope the information in *Break the Bipolar Cycle* will help you build an effective treatment team, so that you can have the support you deserve and need. Too often people with BSD end up going it alone. Family members and health-care providers can sometimes blame the patient (or themselves) for the difficulties caused by BSD. Different and sometimes inaccurate beliefs about the nature of the condition or the course of treatment can lead to arguments and undermine support. But it doesn't have to be that way, and we will provide you with the information you need to help get everyone on the same page.

About the Book

Part 1 provides you with up-to-date information on BSD. The chapters show you how to find yourself in the diagnostic criteria and share the latest information on the neurobiology of BSD and on the currently available medical treatments.

Part 2 addresses the effects of BSD on your life. The chapters illustrate the specific ways in which problems in information processing and mood regulation affect your ability to get started and stay focused, to feel comfortable around people, and to stay well. We provide tools you can use to counter these problems.

Throughout the chapters are exercises to help you manage the difficulties. The exercises come with forms to guide you. In each chapter, we illustrate how to use the forms. There are versions you can copy for your own use in the back of the book.

Think of these exercises and forms as a way in which we can leave the confines of these pages and interact with you. We can't be there with you day in and day out, but we can give you information and guide you to develop skills you need to get better. These exercises give you the self-knowledge you need to break the cycle.

The exercises will help you to uncover things you may not have known about yourself and BSD, and they can help you to be more systematic in your evaluation of your own condition. It is easy to get overwhelmed by BSD. But keeping track of your stressors and symptoms will help you keep your eye on the larger picture, recognizing your own progress and figuring out what you need to optimize your recovery.

You don't have to be perfect in filling out the forms. Even a little information can go a long way toward clarifying the situation. And you don't have to do it alone; you can fill out the forms with a friend or family member or take the forms along to your doctor's office and fill them out together.

Getting control of BSD is a collaborative process. Your doctor can't do it alone, and neither can you. Working through the exercises can help you build a common language to communicate your symptoms and concerns to your doctors and your family and friends. Together, we can break the bipolar cycle and get BSD under control.

How to Use This Book

■ **For a quick start to symptom management.** Up front, in Part 1, we provide a lot of detailed information about BSD. If you want to get practical very quickly, you might want to read Chapter 1 to make sure you understand your diagnosis. Then you can skip right to Part 2, Chapter 6 for information on the effects of BSD on motivation. After this, you can work through the exercises in the chapters in Part 2. If you discover that you need more information, you can go back to Part 1. We will direct you back to the specific chapters you may find helpful.

■ **As a guide to understanding BSD.** If you want more detailed information about the disorder and the process of diagnosis and treatment, then we recommend that you read through the entire book from start to finish. Chapters 1, 2, 3, 6, and 7 can be particularly helpful for family members and friends. These chapters can help your loved ones to understand what's happening and to consider ways to provide support. References for the information in each of the chapters are included in the back of the book.

■ **As a way to start a conversation with your doctor and your family.** You may not identify with every case example in this book. We include stories from patients with different disorders along the bipolar spectrum. But you can use these examples as a way to start a conversation with your doctor or your family members, even if the conversation starts, "I don't feel exactly like that, but I do feel . . ." The case examples are meant to illustrate an idea and to help you compare and contrast your own symptoms to make it easier to talk things over with other people.

Acknowledgments

Many people helped work on this book. Most important, I would like to thank all the patients who helped me learn about bipolar disorder, volunteered their stories, read drafts, and in general kept me focused on getting the book done. I would also like to acknowledge the help of my friend and mentor, Frances Mas, M.D., who has taught me so much about bipolar disorder and made a difference in the lives of so many people. Susanna Goldstein, M.D., has been an invaluable contributor, making insightful comments on the draft and collaborating on many cases. My little sister, Dr. Sheila Nirenberg, of the Department of Physiology and Biophysics at Weill Medical College of Cornell University, spent many enjoyable hours teaching me the basics of neurobiology. Jeremy Coplan, M.D., of SUNY Downstate Medical Center, Richard Lane, M.D., of the University of Arizona, and Robin Wellington, Ph.D., of St. John's University, provided thoughtful comments and helpful advice about the neurobiology sections. Any mistakes in the presentation are mine, not theirs. Bezalel Ron Eichler, Ph.D., contributed excellent ideas throughout the book. Lynn Clemow, Ph.D., provided great suggestions and lots of encouragement. Brent Chabus, M.D., Cynthia Perry, M.D., Serge Sevy, M.D., and Ron Winchel, M.D., are compassionate and knowledgeable psychiatrists, and I have benefitted greatly from working with them. Pamela Plate volunteered to help with the manuscript, and I benefited from her insightful suggestions and helpful corrections. Melissa Weinstein worked diligently to assemble the scientific literature reviewed in this book. My department chairperson, Raymond DiGiuseppe, Ph.D., and my dean, Jeffrey Fagen, Ph.D., at St. John's University have been the source of ongoing support and guidance. Our editor, John Aherne, has been helpful and encouraging throughout. My mother, Edna Nirenberg, and my aunt, Martha Bernstein, taught me to care about words and writing. The entire Brondolo family, and in particular, my father-in-law, Anthony Brondolo, has been endlessly caring and generous. And without my coauthor, Xavier Amador, Ph.D., this book would never have been written.

My father, Jesse S. Nirenberg, Ph.D., deserves credit for starting this whole process. He was the first psychologist I knew.

—Elizabeth Brondolo

I am grateful first and foremost to my patients living with bipolar and related disorders. Their persistence and openness have inspired me to never stop learning about how we can work together more effectively to break the bipolar cycle and make recovery a reality. I also have close friends with these disorders and have learned much about the challenges created by the illness and the important role loved ones can play in recovery. I am grateful for all they have taught me.

Many of the lessons learned in this book came not only from my experiences as a therapist and a loved one but also as a scientist. I want to especially thank the National Institute of Mental Health, the Stanley Research Foundation, and the National Alliance for Research on Schizophrenia and Affective Disorders, which have funded my research on bipolar disorder. Although this research has focused primarily on the problem of poor insight into illness—this book is instead for those with bipolar disorder who understand they have an illness—it taught me much about the obstacles all people with these illnesses face.

Finally, I want to thank Liz Brondolo. In most respects this book is hers. Not only because she did the lion's share of the work, but also because it embodies her experience, expertise, sensitivities, and heart. I am honored to be her coauthor and hope that this book will help people with bipolar spectrum disorders and their loved ones find new ways to work together to rise above the problems created by these illnesses and, ultimately, to recover.

—Xavier Amador

Part 1

The Big Questions

1

How Do I Know That I Have a Bipolar Spectrum Disorder?

Understanding the Diagnosis

KEY POINTS

Bipolar spectrum disorders include several different conditions, including bipolar I, bipolar II, bipolar NOS, and cyclothymia.

All the conditions involve mood cycling.

The symptoms include a broader range of difficulties than just changes in mood.

Bipolar spectrum disorders are much more common than previously recognized.

It can be hard to accept the diagnosis, but understanding and accepting the BSD diagnosis are essential to the process of recovery.

Getting the correct diagnosis of bipolar spectrum disorder is the first step. Studies have shown (and most patients know) that getting the right diagnosis can be challenging, with many different doctors and specialists offering their different opinions and diagnoses. In fact, the average length of time from when you first approach a doctor to when you get a correct diagnosis is about ten years! So if you are finally getting the right diagnosis, you are on your way to recovery.

But you may still have some questions. Do you really have BSD? Maybe the original diagnoses were right? Maybe you really have depression or personality problems or some other condition?

A diagnosis including the words *bipolar disorder* can seem strange and scary. If you have had classic symptoms, like big mood swings or a clear-cut episode of mania where you ended up in the hospital, the diagnosis may make sense to you. If you are like the majority of people with BSD, however, your symptoms may not seem to match traditional ideas of bipolar disorder.

As you will learn, the bipolar spectrum includes conditions with a broad range of symptoms. These symptoms can vary in the way they are expressed in everyday life and in their intensity, making them hard to recognize. But when you can recognize the symptoms, the picture becomes clearer—and then the treatment options become clearer as well. And much more effective.

Why Is It So Important to Learn About BSD?

The more you know, the more you can recognize and track your symptoms; in turn this will help you understand your diagnosis and work with your treatment team to optimize your treatment. Unlike many medical disorders that are diagnosed with a blood test or other biological markers, BSD symptoms need to be recognized and reported by you (and probably your friends and family as well).

Think about the difference between diagnosing diabetes and diagnosing migraine headaches. For diabetes, the diagnosis is based on a blood test. But for migraine, the diagnosis is based on the doctor's observations and on the patient's self-report of symptoms.

The same thing holds true for BSD. There are currently no physical tests that help establish a definitive diagnosis. Instead, the doctor makes his or her own observations and collects information from you and those who know you. Your doctor may use diagnostic interviews, observations, and paper-and-pencil surveys to gather all this information.

To make a diagnosis of BSD, the doctor needs information not only about your current difficulties but also about your history—the history of your symptoms and your overall functioning. After all, it's a cycling disorder. So the symptoms you have now (when you are in the doctor's office getting a diagnosis) may not be the same symptoms you have had at other times during different cycles.

Your doctor also may want to ask questions of your family and/or friends. In certain cycles of the disorder, especially periods of mania or hypomania, you may not be a perfect reporter of your symptoms. In fact, part of what makes the diagnosis so difficult is that individuals with BSD often do not perceive their moods as any more cyclical than other people's moods. And when you are sick, you may not accurately remember the symptoms you have had at other times. You might think, "I feel awful now, and I have always felt this way." Your family and friends may provide a different perspective.

Your doctor needs to know about your family's health history as well, because bipolar disorders have a strong genetic component. Your doctor may also ask about other conditions, including depression, substance abuse problems, or anxiety disorders. The doctor may also ask about relatives with severe anger problems or who were big risk takers.

But the more you know, the more accurate you can be in giving a clear picture of your symptoms. And the better you are at recognizing the symptoms, the easier it is to get BSD under control. So we hope you will take time to get a little more familiar with the diagnosis and that you will share your knowledge with your family and friends as well. The more they know, the better they will be able to work with you and your doctor.

Historical Context

Let's start with some historical context. Bipolar disorder used to be called manic depression, or manic-depressive illness. Doctors, and the public at large, generally believed that the primary symptoms were mood swings: periods of very up, excited, or elated moods (called mania) alternating with periods of very low moods (called depression). In between, doctors assumed that mood and functioning were essentially normal. Bipolar disorder was assumed to be different from major depression and to be very rare.

What you may not have known is that today clinicians and researchers are challenging these old assumptions. And the new ways doctors are thinking about bipolar disorder can help make the diagnosis and treatment much more straightforward. So let's look at some of these ideas.

One Disorder or Many?

Research suggests that there are more conditions that fall under the bipolar spectrum than just classic manic-depressive illness or bipolar I. Instead, it may be better to think of *bipolar spectrum disorders* as a group of related conditions that range in symptoms and severity. Scientists are still debating exactly which disorders should be grouped together as part of the bipolar spectrum. Table 1.1 lists various disorders that may be part of the bipolar spectrum, as well as some related conditions. As you will see later in this chapter, the disorders all have cycling moods in common—but there are differ-

Table 1.1 Bipolar Spectrum Diagnoses and Prevalence

Diagnoses	Lifetime Prevalence Across National and International Studies*
Bipolar I	0.3–1.7% (about 3–7 million in the United States)
Bipolar II	0.3–1.6% (about 1.75 million in the United States)
Cyclothymia	About 1%
Bipolar Spectrum Disorders (covering a range of symptoms and severity)	3–8.3%
Other possible diagnoses and related conditions:	
Schizoaffective disorder	About 0.5%
Borderline personality disorder	About 2%
Bipolar III (not an official DSM-IV diagnosis)	3–10% of individuals diagnosed with depression

*International studies indicate lifetime prevalence rates for all mood disorders, including depression, range from 7% to 19%.

ences in the specific nature of the symptoms. From this point forward, unless we are specifically talking about one of these disorders, when we use the term *BSDs*, we are referring to all of them—to the spectrum.

The American Psychiatric Association's *Diagnostic and Statistical Manual of Mental Disorders* (*DSM-IV-TR*), the manual that healthcare providers use to guide their diagnoses of patients, includes a section on mood disorders. This section provides guidelines for diagnosing both unipolar depression and bipolar disorder. Unipolar depression (depression without mania) is what major depression is called. The old way of thinking about mood disorders made a clear separation between bipolar disorder and major depression. Unipolar depression was a diagnosis given to people with depression only—they had no manic symptoms. Bipolar depression was reserved for people who had experienced clear hypomanic or manic symptoms, either alone or along with their depressive symptoms. People with these manic or hypomanic symptoms were considered to have a very different disorder (and in some ways a more stigmatized disorder) than people who "just" had depression. But doctors are now realizing that the characteristics of some types of unipolar depression and bipolar disorder may overlap more than they recognized before.

Many leading researchers are suggesting that it may be more accurate to think about a broader spectrum of mood disorders in which the important consideration is the cycling nature of the symptoms. In this model, recurrent (also called cycling, or episodic) mood disorders are all linked together, whether the recurrences, or cycles, involve symptoms of depression or mania. So some researchers have suggested that it may be more appropriate to think about a *recurrent mood disorders spectrum* that includes both the bipolar spectrum disorders as well as recurrent depressions. (For a very good discussion of the mood disorders spectrum, you may want to check out *Why Am I Still Depressed?*, a book by Dr. Jim Phelps.)

Why does it matter if it's a *spectrum* of mood disorders? Because thinking about a spectrum helps you understand the different symptoms that you have. You don't have to be supermanic (e.g., spending wildly or talking a blue streak) to have some elements of bipolar disorder. If you understand the underlying nature of the disorders, the changes in mood, thinking, and behavior that accompany BSDs, then you can detect even low levels of the key symptoms. And this will help you get better, more appropriate, and effective treatment.

Once a wider range of symptoms was identified, it became much clearer that bipolar spectrum disorders were much more common than doctors had previously realized. If you look at Table 1.1, you will see that all together, using a broader set of diagnostic criteria, as much as 8 percent of the population may have a BSD over the course of their lifetime. Bipolar I probably affects about 1 to 2 percent of the population, or about three to seven million Americans. Depending on the estimates, between 1 and 3 percent of Americans are likely to have bipolar II or cyclothymia. Using strict criteria, the most recent studies suggest a lifetime prevalence of almost 3 to 4 percent for BSDs. But other new studies from Europe and the United States, which use a broader definition of BSD, suggest that from 6.4 to more than 8 percent of the population have, over the course of their lifetimes, met criteria for a bipolar spectrum disorder.

Two others disorders, borderline personality disorder and schizo-affective disorder, may be related to bipolar disorder. Borderline personality disorder is a condition that also involves chronic mood instability. Schizoaffective disorder is a condition in which the symptoms are similar to BSD, but the patients display psychotic symptoms between mood episodes. Recurrent depression may affect still more individuals.

What's the bottom line? Many people are affected by BSD and related disorders. Even if you take a conservative estimate, about one out of every twenty-five people may have a bipolar spectrum disorder over the course of their lifetime. That's a lot of people. If you have BSD, you are not alone.

Beyond the Mood Episodes

Doctors are also now realizing that bipolar disorder comes with more symptoms than just mood swings. These symptoms sometimes persist, even between mood swings and even when you are taking your medicine. Individuals with BSD may also exhibit the following symptoms:

- Longer-term problems with mood quality (symptoms of depression even when the individual is not in a major depression)
- Difficulties with mood regulation and stability (a very changeable or sensitive mood even when the individual is not acutely manic or depressed)
- Problems with information processing (difficulties with organizing, remembering, and paying attention)
- Problems with sleep quality and with circadian rhythms (daily cycles of waking, energy, and sleep)

These symptoms deserve attention, too. As you get better at recognizing and monitoring these symptoms, you will be able to work with your treatment team to develop treatment strategies to manage the episodes and the between-episode symptoms as well.

What Are the Symptoms?

All the bipolar spectrum disorders share a core feature: there is a noticeable shift in mood, thinking, and activity during the course of the illness.

Depending on the specific diagnosis, the disorders involve symptoms that are associated with episodes of mania, hypomania, depression, and/or a mixed state. In the next sections, we will describe each of these episodes and the conditions in a little detail, but you should be aware that there are differences of opinion about the exact symptoms that are associated with each diagnosis. We use a broad list, including symptoms identified by both U.S. and European researchers, because we think you may be more likely to "find yourself" in these descriptions. Your best bet is to think through your symptoms using the exercises in Chapter 3. If you can, talk the symptoms and diagnosis over with a family member or friend to get further information and their input. Then review your list with your doctor.

Describing the Symptoms

Let's start by talking about the characteristics of each type of cycling episode. Although we often talk as if the mood is the only thing that counts, these episodes affect your thinking, as well as your activity levels and behavior. In fact, leading scientists think that the most important distinguishing characteristic is really the activity level, not the quality of the mood. So for each type of episode, we will describe the symptoms associated with your mood and energy, your thinking, and your activity or behavior.

Mania and Hypomania. In the following paragraphs, we list symptoms of mania and hypomania. Hypomania means "less than mania"—so fewer or less intense manic symptoms may constitute hypomania. The *DSM-IV-TR* list of symptoms associated with a manic episode includes an "abnormally and persistently elevated, expansive, or irritable mood," as well as "inflated self-esteem or grandiosity," "decreased need for sleep," "more talkative than usual," "flight of ideas or subjective experience of racing thoughts," "distractibility," "increase in goal-directed activity," and "excessive involvement in pleasurable activities that have a high potential for painful consequences."

We will spend the next few paragraphs describing these symptoms in "lay language," the way people describe these symptoms to us. You will notice that many of these symptoms, in their early stages, simply look like high-energy normal behavior. They are not readily identifiable as symptoms.

This is part of the reason why it can be hard to identify symptoms as manic or hypomanic. But you can start to think about your moods, thinking, or behavior as symptoms if they represent a notice-able change from the way you usually feel or if they are so intense that they are noticeable to others and create difficulties or danger in your life. You might think about your mood, thinking, and behavior as symptoms of a BSD if you can say things like, "When I felt like that, other people asked me why I was being so. . . ."

Or you look back and say, "Wow, I was thinking so quickly and acting so [impulsively or irritably], and then I got into so much trouble at work." Or, "I felt so good for a while, and then I fell apart and got so depressed again."

■ **Mood and Energy.** In the early stages of a manic, or "up," cycle, you may feel great, euphoric, or elated. It may seem like you *finally* feel good. You may need less sleep than usual. You may feel "juiced up," electric with energy and ideas—or you may feel very irritable or angry, losing your temper at the slightest provocation.

As the episode progresses, you are more likely to feel rage or intense distress or even some of the feelings you usually label as depression. You may feel full of energy even when you get very little rest. You may feel very sexual, full of desire—or you may feel attracted to many people.

■ **Thinking.** Mania and hypomania are reflected in your thinking as well. Your thoughts may race, your ideas may seem especially creative, and you may feel superconfident. Initially, you may be able to make more rapid connections than you used to (or than other people can). You may feel (and be) more creative.

But these racing thoughts may also make you distractible, so you end up jumping from topic to topic. Your speech may seem pressured or rapid, and you may make lots of puns or jokes.

You may find a change in the way you use words, so that you enjoy the sounds of different interesting words or enjoy saying different words together. Your judgment may be impaired, making you overly optimistic about plans or ideas or unable to see yourself clearly.

As the mania progresses, you may think so quickly that you can't fully form your ideas. If mania is untreated, you may show symptoms of psychosis. You may make connections between topics that aren't so clear to other people. You may have hallucinations or delusions, and you may have difficulty distinguishing dreams from reality. Your judgment may be impaired. As mania progresses, you may not be able to perceive more serious risks, and you may put yourself in harm's way—physically, financially, or personally.

■ **Activity and Behavior.** Initially, you may be more active—working more, traveling more, and moving around more. You may engage in more high-risk behaviors—spending more, drinking or eating more, using drugs, or having more sexual activity. As the mania progresses, you may become a whirlwind of physical activity, in constant motion.

The clinical picture is not the same for everyone. Initially, some people may have expansive behavior, becoming the life of the party or superproductive for a short while. Others may feel driven to engage in risky but pleasurable behavior (for example, drug use or shopping sprees). Others may fly off the handle, quickly becoming enraged or battling with everyone.

In the early stages, other people can mistake the symptoms of mania for confidence, daring, creativity, and sexual charisma. The expression of irritability and anger or impatience can sometimes be interpreted as a show of power: "He must be a big shot, if he can boss people around like that." If these characteristics intensify and are accompanied by an inability to function normally, it may be worth considering that they could be symptoms of hypomania or mania. And when mania develops, it may be necessary for you to be treated in a hospital for safety.

Depression. Patients with BSD may have both major and minor depression. Again, minor depression, or dysthymia, entails fewer, shorter, or less intense symptoms of depression. The *DSM-IV-TR* list of symptoms associated with a depressive episode include a "depressed mood most of the day," "markedly diminished interest or pleasure in all or almost all activities," "significant weight loss, when not dieting, or weight gain," insomnia or hypersomnia," "psychomotor agitation and retardation," "fatigue or loss of energy," "feelings of worthlessness or excessive or inappropriate guilt," "diminished ability to think or concentrate or indecisiveness," and "recurrent thoughts of death." Depression in bipolar disorder may have some different symptoms than depression that has been associated with unipolar depression. The distinguishing features are not clear or completely consistent, but they may include a tendency to sleep more (rather than sleep less), to have more marked changes in activity and mood over the course of the day, and to have even lower levels of activity.

■ **Mood and Energy.** During a depressive episode, you may feel slow or sad, or you may feel almost nothing at all, as if you are numb or empty. You may feel as if you can't move, can't concentrate, can't think—as if any kind of energy or kick has been sucked right out of you. Some people have difficulty sleeping, while others sleep too much. Your appetite may decrease or increase.

■ **Thinking.** Your thinking may become more rigid and more negative. You may develop more catastrophic ideas—a temporary setback becomes a permanent failure. You may make connections between ideas or information, but the connections lead to negative conclusions, even in the face of logic. You may believe you are irreparably damaged and your future is bleak. You may be especially sensitive to criticism. You may feel overwhelming guilt. Often people think about death or about killing themselves.

■ **Activity and Behavior.** You may be much less active and feel less able to do the things you should do. You may move much more slowly—just getting off the couch may seem like an overwhelming chore. In bipolar depression (depression that occurs when people have BSD), you may feel as if you have "leaden paralysis," you just can't move. But again, the clinical picture is not the same for everyone. In some cases, people can feel and look very restless and agitated. This is part of why it can be difficult to distinguish between an agitated state of depression and an agitated mania or mixed state.

Mixed State. Some individuals with bipolar disorder experience a mixed state. A mixed state occurs when you have symptoms of both depression and mania or hypomania at the same time.

■ **Mood and Energy.** You can show or feel the energy and/or intensity of mania, but the quality of your mood is negative. You may experience a tense energy or a restless exhaustion; that is, you may feel exhausted but look agitated or look exhausted but feel agitated. Anger and irritability are also common markers of a mixed state. Sometimes it can seem as if there is an electric edge to your anger. The anger may be turned toward yourself, and you may feel particularly self-hating.

■ **Thinking.** You may seem very slowed down but feel as if your thoughts are racing. You may be especially prone to having repetitive thoughts, particularly about situations that distress you. You may have the energy to keep moving and interacting with other people, but every interaction feels as if it cuts with a knife. Your skin feels too thin. Sometimes a mixed state is accompanied by very vivid and scary dreams or images.

■ **Activity and Behavior.** The patterns of activity can be varied in this state. The behavior will depend on your energy level, but it is not uncommon for people to feel unable to engage in productive activities during this time.

Altogether a mixed state is particularly uncomfortable. Because of the combination of symptoms, people are at increased risk for attempting suicide when they are in a mixed state compared with other periods.

BSD Diagnosis

How does your doctor decide that you have a bipolar spectrum disorder? If you have ever had symptoms of hypomania or mania, you are likely to get a bipolar spectrum diagnosis. The different bipolar disorders vary in the intensity and duration that symptoms of mania are displayed. (You might be wondering why it's so hard to make the diagnosis of BSD, if all it takes is the presence of manic symptoms. As you are beginning to see, it can be hard to recognize symptoms of mania. There are big individual differences in the way people show manic symptoms, and it can be hard to identify them against the backdrop of your life.)

Bipolar I diagnoses have three parts. The first part requires that the doctor indicate the type of disorder (that is, bipolar disorder versus another kind of disorder). The second part requires that the doctor indicate the nature of the last episode (manic, depressed, mixed, or other). And the third part requires that the doctor indicate the severity of the condition.

If you have ever had a full manic or mixed episode that lasted for seven days without treatment, you will get a diagnosis of bipolar disorder I. The last two parts of the diagnosis require an ongoing diagnostic process. If your mood symptoms change, the last two parts of your diagnosis will change as well. So if your first episode was manic but your most recent episode involved a mixed state, your diagnosis changes to reflect the change in symptoms.

If you have had an episode of hypomania and have also had one or more episodes of depression, both of which cause an impairment in functioning or a noticeable change in behavior, you will get a diagnosis of bipolar II. Evidence of mania-related symptoms for four days is enough to justify a classification of the symptoms as hypomania. However, many researchers and clinicians argue that the presence of these symptoms for two days should probably be regarded as indicating hypomania. And some doctors suggest that even briefer periods should be used to identify a period of hypomania. Older people may be more likely to have brief hypomanic or manic episodes.

If you have symptoms of mania that do not meet the full criteria for a manic episode as well as symptoms of depression that do not last long enough or aren't severe enough to meet the criteria for a depressive episode, you will get a diagnosis of cyclothymia. If you have a cycling mood disorder but your symptoms only match those of depression, then you may get a diagnosis of major depressive disorder, recurrent.

Sometimes your symptoms just don't quite fit the pattern. You may have intense but very rapid cycling symptoms that do not last as long or aren't quite the same as described in the diagnostic manuals. Then your doctor may give you a diagnosis of BSD not otherwise specified (NOS). For example, if you have symptoms of bipolar II or cyclothymia but you don't seem to have experienced significant consequences (for example, you have not lost a job or been unable to work or been in trouble in some way), these symptoms are referred to as "soft" bipolar. This just means the symptoms can be harder to recognize or an individual symptom can be less severe. But overall the disorder is still hard on you. Any bipolar spectrum disorder can interfere with your life. This is the case even if all the symptoms are not there and even if some of the symptoms don't seem very severe.

You can expect that there will be changes in the diagnostic terms and criteria as new findings emerge. Now that it is more accepted that there are a range of bipolar spectrum disorders, doctors and scientists will work to distinguish more clearly among these disorders. And as the diagnostic process improves, researchers will be better able to test ideas about the underlying causes and best treatments for each bipolar spectrum disorder.

Case Studies

Let's look at some specific cases to get the feel of what these symptoms look like in real life. You might notice that all these cases have symptoms that overlap. The symptoms also overlap with those resulting from other mental health problems. These patients could have been (and were) diagnosed with other conditions at different times in their lives. The difficulties in making a correct diagnosis slowed down the process of recovery. Once the diagnosis was correct, however, we could start effective treatment.

Frank's Story

Frank is a sixty-five-year-old man. Up until five years ago, he was working more than full time. For long periods, he could travel to different cities and work "full steam ahead" for five or ten days straight. He needed very little sleep, and he felt like his mind worked like lightning. He could think quickly and easily move from one task to another. But sometimes he would crawl into bed unable to do anything for days on end. His wife would have to cover all his responsibilities and sometimes cancel his appointments.

Recently, he had an episode when he believed he could do anything and "fired" his bosses. He spent thousands of dollars buying expensive items, staying in expensive hotels, and racing from one section of the country to the other.

Frank is a classic case of bipolar I. This is because he had a full-blown manic episode with symptoms of grandiosity, decreased need for sleep, as well as excessive involvement in pleasurable activities that have a high potential for painful consequences.

Frank's diagnosis is bipolar disorder I, most recent episode manic, severe.

Marisol's Story

Marisol had symptoms of anxiety and some depression through her childhood and teen years. After college, she decided to go back to get more education. Over a period of time, she developed an intense passion for her classes. She believed she would someday become a great biologist, developing new treatments and traveling the world to cure people. She believed she was "born again" from the new knowledge she was gaining in school. She began to talk very quickly and intensely.

At the same time, she developed a severe hypochondriasis, believing she had the Asian flu or other medical disorders. She called 911 repeatedly to get emergency help. Once she was well treated, the symptoms of hypochondriasis disappeared. But she didn't come to see me until she was in a serious depression.

Marisol has also been diagnosed with bipolar I. What symptoms did Marisol display? During her manic episode, she had symptoms of racing thoughts, pressured speech, and grandiosity. Her judgment about her own condition was severely impaired. More recently, she has had symptoms of depression, including difficulty sleeping, trouble concentrating, and a depressed mood.

Marisol's diagnosis is bipolar disorder I, most recent episode depressed, severe.

Janine's Story

When she first came to see me, Janine displayed symptoms of depression most of the time: she was fatigued, felt very much like a failure, and had no interest in any of her previous activities. She felt sad and low, and she had a great deal of difficulty concentrating and initiating purposeful work.

But in the past Janine had symptoms of hypomania. When she was younger, she was a little grandiose, very much a thrill seeker and risk taker, and very, very actively engaged in career-directed activities. Janine worked in the entertainment business. Staying out at parties and running around was part of her professional life. She had a "larger-than-life" personality and was always pushing nonstop to succeed. At the time, these characteristics probably didn't strike anyone in her industry as hypomanic. Now, in between periods of depression, she will occasionally show symptoms of hypomania again, becoming hypersexual and very irritable and impatient.

I diagnosed Janine with bipolar II because she has had many recurrent depressive episodes, but she has also experienced episodes of hypomania. She never had a clearly recognizable manic episode.

Janine's diagnosis is bipolar disorder II.

Your Diagnosis

And now for the most important case study: you. Let's make sure you are aware of your own diagnosis. If you don't know the exact nature of your diagnosis, be sure to ask your doctor for a full explanation, and have a friend or loved one come with you when your doctor explains it to you. It is worth understanding the details, and it will help to have someone there with you in order to fully understand the diagnosis and ask the questions you may not think to ask. Getting it right directs the nature of your treatment.

As we will discuss in more detail in the next chapter, you may have one or more other diagnoses in addition to BSD. About 70 percent of individuals with BSD have a co-occurring psychiatric disorder. The most common disorders that occur along with BSD are problems with substance abuse, anxiety, or attention deficit disorder.

Knowing Your Diagnosis

Try writing your diagnosis in Exercise 1 at the end of this chapter. Ask your doctor to tell you what symptoms made him or her decide the diagnosis was a bipolar spectrum disorder. Write down those symptoms as well. Although it can be hard to accept that you have BSD, it can be really helpful to know your diagnosis.

Some people feel very relieved when they find out they have a BSD. They have been suffering and unable to understand why things are so difficult for them. It is a relief to get some answers. And of course, once they are treated effectively, it is an even bigger relief to feel better.

On the other hand, sometimes our patients feel very angry with us when we give them a diagnosis in the bipolar spectrum. When we give them the diagnosis, they feel convinced it means that we think they are crazy or bad or damaged goods. They feel as if we "gave" them bipolar, when what we gave them was the diagnosis.

Here are some of the thoughts our patients have had when we talked about the diagnosis of bipolar spectrum disorder:

- "Bipolar disorder! I am really crazy. Things are hopeless. I'll never have a life."
- "I was fine before you told me I had bipolar."
- "I would have gotten better, if you hadn't told me I had bipolar."
- "No! I just need more discipline or more self-esteem."
- "If only I had the right insight into my past, all my symptoms would go away."

All our patients have felt unprepared to take on the challenge of managing a medical disorder like bipolar. You may feel the same way. You can't imagine what you will need to do to manage BSD.

After all, you didn't plan on getting sick. You may have thought, "Oh, sometime in the future I might have heart disease like my grandfather," or maybe, "I wouldn't be surprised if I had an episode of depression." But it's a good bet that you didn't think you would end up with bipolar disorder. No one asks for BSD, and no one wants it. But sometimes it happens. And you can develop a plan to manage it.

Developing a Plan

The first step to developing a plan is to accept that you have a medical condition with symptoms that require attention. The symptoms are tough, but they can be managed. It takes hard work and patience. But you already know that the most satisfying things in life come when you make an investment and work to master the challenges involved. That's as true in bipolar disorder as it is in sports or science or art. No one gets to be a successful player without plenty of hours of practice. And no one gets to be a successful player without facing some tough times and overcoming them.

In BSD strength and success come from steady, inventive hard work. Your progress is helped by good teamwork. So each of the following chapters will help you consider what it takes to succeed and how to get your team assembled and in action. You can do it.

EXERCISE 1
Clarifying Your Diagnosis

Write down your diagnosis. It will be easier to manage this disorder
if you are straightforward and clear about what the difficulties are.
If you own your condition, you can begin to manage it.

Your bipolar spectrum diagnosis: ....

Other diagnoses: ....

Additional medical conditions: ....

Ask your doctor what the specific symptoms were that led to the
diagnosis of bipolar disorder. Write them here.

Symptoms: ....

....

....

....

A Note on Proper Diagnosis

After reading a draft of this chapter, a patient, Samantha, asked us
to discuss one other issue. She appreciated the need to accept and
understand the diagnosis, but she felt very uncomfortable about the
way a bipolar diagnosis is handled in the news media. She pointed
out that there is so much bad news attached to bipolar disorder these
days—it seems as if anyone who gets caught doing anything illegal
or dangerous is suddenly diagnosed with bipolar disorder.

Samantha wanted to make sure that we communicated two things that are important. First, having bipolar disorder is very difficult. No one who actually has BSD wants it just so they can have an excuse for bad behavior. Second, just because people have BSD doesn't mean they are criminals. It doesn't mean they will act in a lawless or dangerous way. It is hard enough to manage the disorder without having to worry that everyone else will think you are either faking it or are about to go wild.

She hoped that we would encourage people to speak up about their BSD. She wanted us to point out that people with BSD, like everyone else, sometimes make mistakes, sometimes have bad judgment, but mostly are just trying to figure out how to manage a challenging condition and get on with their lives. With greater understanding and better public awareness, early detection will help people avoid some of the consequences of untreated BSD.

In Chapter 2 we will talk about why it is so hard to get a correct diagnosis and how you can use your understanding of BSD and its symptoms to regain control of your life. In Chapter 3 you will get some practice recognizing your own BSD symptoms and matching them to symptom categories the doctors use to make the diagnosis.

Notes for the Family

As you discuss the issues related to diagnosis and family history of BSD, you may feel uncomfortable. It can be a strange idea to consider yourself or your family members through the lens of BSD. It can be upsetting to think "Maybe Uncle Bob's rages were really symptoms of BSD" or "Maybe my difficulties finishing school were related to BSD."

You may feel defensive and nervous, or maybe even a little attacked, as your family member with BSD works to review his or her family history. But it is still worth doing. It can help everyone be a little more clinical about the situation. And no one gets BSD from reviewing symptoms.

You don't want to turn every piece of behavior into a BSD symptom or see every argument as evidence of BSD. But it can be helpful to learn about BSD symptoms and to be willing to talk about these symptoms in an open way.

Is It Really BSD?

Common Diagnostic Dilemmas

KEY POINTS

It can be difficult to make the diagnosis of BSD.

Symptoms can look like another condition.

Symptoms can seem like part of one's personality.

Most people have more than one condition.

Frank was originally given the diagnosis of major depression. He cycled through episodes of hypomania and depression for more than fifteen years before he had his first manic episode. Finally, at age sixty, he had a major manic episode, and the diagnosis became a little clearer.

Lucia was originally diagnosed with ADHD when she was eight. She was treated with Ritalin, which made some of the symptoms better and others worse. Finally, at age sixteen, she was diagnosed with BSD and treated successfully with lithium.

Chris, aged forty-five, was treated for major depression and substance abuse for ten years before he received a correct diagnosis of bipolar II and was started on lithium.

Emily, aged fifty, was diagnosed with OCD (obsessive-compulsive disorder) and major depression. But she just never seemed to get better. Finally, she received a diagnosis of BSD as well as OCD.

The Struggle for an Accurate Diagnosis

It can be difficult to make a diagnosis of BSD. In fact, the chances are that BSD isn't the first diagnosis you received from a mental health provider. Studies have shown (and most patients know) that getting the right diagnosis can be challenging. Some research suggests that up to 50 percent of individuals who eventually are correctly diagnosed with a BSD were first incorrectly diagnosed with depression.

Why is it so confusing? The causes for the underlying disorder are not yet known, and there are no standard tests of brain functioning that can diagnose BSD. The disorder comes with a broader range of symptoms than initially recognized. The symptoms wax and wane over time. At any one point in time, it can be hard to determine exactly what the diagnosis should be: major depressive disorder? bipolar I? attention deficit disorder? or some other choice entirely?

So it isn't surprising that it may have been difficult for you to get an accurate diagnosis. It can be useful to consider what might go wrong along the way to a correct diagnosis. This can help you evaluate your own symptoms and make sure you and your doctor are on the right track. And it may help you put your own treatment history into perspective. Let's look at some common issues that arise during the initial process of diagnosis.

BSD or Major Depression?

Symptoms of depression in BSD are much more frequent and more distressing than doctors previously realized. And depressive symptoms are more common than the cardinal symptoms of mania (for example, a very elevated mood or reckless behavior) that would trigger a diagnosis of BSD.

In one study, scientists asked people with BSD to keep track of their symptoms every week for several months. They found that people reported having symptoms in about half the weeks. For most of those weeks, the symptoms were symptoms of depression. Other studies have found that more than 80 percent of relapses in BSD appear to involve depression. In addition, when people go to the doctor for help, they are more likely to go when they are in distress. (People rarely come to see me to get treatment when they feel the elated or positive moods they may experience in hypomania or mania.) This means the symptoms of depression may be much more obvious to you and your doctors than some of the other difficulties you are experiencing.

And here is where the difficulty lies. The treatments for depression can sometimes make bipolar worse. You may be depressed and have major depressive disorder. But it is also worth considering that you may have depression in the context of BSD or you may be in a mixed state as part of bipolar I. That is why it is important to consider all your symptoms, including signs of excess energy, hypersexuality, or racing thoughts. Your symptoms may not perfectly match the *DSM-IV-TR* diagnostic criteria, but if you suspect they may be signs of a mixed state or if you think you have had a manic or hypomanic episode, share your thoughts with your doctor. Together, you can evaluate the meaning of the symptoms.

May's Story. May first presented with severe depressive symptoms when she was a teenager. She couldn't get out of bed, she couldn't go to school, she wanted to die. She was hospitalized, given a diagnosis of major depression, and prescribed several different antidepressants. Within two weeks she looked better and was discharged from the hospital. But as she continued to take the antidepressants after her discharge, her condition worsened. She still looked very depressed, but now her thoughts were racing. She began spending money and making elaborate travel arrangements. Her mother had to race to the airport to prevent her from flying off across the country. She went back to the doctor, who was now able to see that May really had BSD, probably bipolar I.

BSD or a Personality Problem?

Is it a personality problem, or are the difficulties really symptoms of BSD? The diagnostic criteria for BSD require that the symptoms must cause changes in behavior that are noticeable to other people. The difficulty is that other people, including close friends and relatives, don't necessarily regard changes in behavior as symptoms. They may think that these actions or attitudes are just aspects of your personality—"That's the way John is. He's always moody."

Or your friends or family may know some of the specific stressors you face and think that your symptoms reflect the way you are handling the situation. Others may have more psychological interpretations of your behavior. They may believe you are angry or irritable or anxious because of personality issues or psychological dynamics— "Joe always gets angry like that because he had a bad relationship with his father." Those things may be true, but the mood and behavior changes can still be symptoms. They are just getting expressed in this particular situation because of your life circumstances.

Because people with BSD have symptoms even when they are not manic or depressed, it can be particularly difficult to distinguish between symptoms and personality characteristics. There are two sets of symptoms, *mood lability* and *interpersonal sensitivity*, that are most likely to be interpreted as personality issues or stress responses. Some researchers have identified these symptoms as being closely associated with BSD, but they are not widely recognized and have not yet been included in the diagnostic manuals.

Mood lability means your mood is very changeable. You may be more sensitive to stress, more likely to cry or get irritable when you are stressed, and also more likely to have transitory moments of joy. When your mood is labile, you might be thinking that you are upset about some recent event or that this is just the way you are, a sensitive person. The people around you may come to accept this part of you, that you are a moody, sensitive person.

It is easier to recognize mood lability as a symptom when it is more severe. In these cases, moods change every few seconds and the facial expressions associated with the moods change rapidly and are very extreme. If you find that your "skin is very thin" (that you are very irritable or are reacting to things quickly and intensely), and that people are noticing it, you might want to consider the idea that you are having the symptom of mood lability.

Heightened interpersonal sensitivity is another symptom common to individuals with some types of BSD. Individuals with heightened interpersonal sensitivity feel very uncomfortable when they are interacting with other people or after they have had a conversation. If you have this symptom, you may feel as if you are hyper-self-aware watching and judging your own actions. You may feel very anxious or angry when you are interacting with others, on guard against criticism. You may find yourself ruminating about conversations that went awry. Sometimes it may seem easier to avoid a conversation than have to face the intense anxiety or agitation afterward. These symptoms can overlap with the symptoms of social anxiety, which can occur along with BSD.

Kelly's Story. Kelly came to my office in a very upset state. She was ruminating over an incident that happened when she was at a party with an acquaintance, Nadia. Nadia deliberately interrupted Kelly while Kelly was telling a story. Then Nadia hijacked the conversation and excluded Kelly from the rest of the conversation. Kelly felt very angry and embarrassed at the time and feels a fresh dose of anger and embarrassment every time she thinks about the situation. She hasn't been able to get it out of her mind for several weeks. No matter how much she talks it over with her friends, she just can't resolve the issue in her mind. She is so distressed by her reaction, she has become afraid to go out socially, because she is concerned she will have a problem and be unable to get over it.

Is this a personality problem or a symptom of obsessive-compulsive disorder? It could go either way. Based on this story alone, it would be hard to determine if Kelly is just thin-skinned or if she was experiencing a more severe problem. But in this case, Kelly had a history of two manic episodes and a longer period of depression. The energy of her thoughts combined with the intensity of her mood suggested that these symptoms might be better considered to be part of a mixed state rather than simply a function of personality problems. I called her psychiatrist, and he prescribed a small dose of an antipsychotic medication that was approved for treating bipolar disorder. Within a very short time, Kelly had a great improvement in her interpersonal sensitivity. She is still sensitive, but now she can socialize without getting as overwhelmed by her concerns.

BSD or a Mood Disorder from Substance Abuse?

Part of the difficulty with diagnosis in BSD is that up to 70 percent of BSD patients also have another psychiatric disorder. One of the most common co-occurring disorders is substance abuse. More than 60 percent of individuals with BSD also have difficulty with alcohol or other drugs, with almost half of all individuals with BSD reporting an alcohol abuse or dependence problem.

Alcohol or drug abuse or dependence can make it difficult to tell whether the symptoms you present are a function of drinking or drug use or of BSD. Like the cycles of BSD, alcohol initially disinhibits you, but then it depresses you. Your emotional reactions can become more intense. It can be very difficult to determine if you are having a problem with depression or mood lability or a problem with alcohol.

In some cases, people with BSD try to self-medicate with alcohol to reduce their symptoms of anxiety or agitation. But it isn't just self-medication. Underlying problems with mood stabilization can also make you more likely to abuse other dangerous drugs. Errors in the regulation of some neurotransmitters in different areas of the brain can make you more likely to pursue pleasurable or exciting activities with no ability to respond to signs of danger. So you may find yourself compelled to binge or to seek excitement, even when you know you are putting yourself in danger. The "danger" messages just don't carry the emotional weight that the "pleasure" messages do.

Very often psychiatrists will be unwilling to treat the BSD until the substance use stops. Although there are good arguments for this approach, it can be very difficult to tolerate the symptoms of BSD, especially if you have been used to self-medicating with drugs or alcohol. It can be helpful to seek out specialists in dual diagnoses (substance abuse and mood disorders). If these specialists are not available in your area, your doctor may be able to get some advice from other doctors through the Internet. You can work closely to contract with your doctor to get some help with your BSD symptoms as you participate actively in substance abuse treatment.

BSD or Anxiety Disorder?

Is it an anxiety disorder? Many individuals with BSD also have anxiety disorders, including panic disorder, agoraphobia, or obsessive-compulsive disorder (OCD). We have found that many of the patients in our groups for BSD have anxiety disorders. And many of the patients in our groups for OCD actually had BSD as well, even though that wasn't obvious from the beginning.

When you are more activated, as you can be during a mixed or manic episode, mild anxiety symptoms can get much worse. It is not uncommon to see patients engaged in nonstop obsessive thinking or compulsive rituals when they are in a mixed state. At any particular visit, this can make it very hard to tell if the symptoms are BSD or anxiety disorders or a combination of the two conditions. This is especially problematic because the treatments for anxiety conditions include antidepressants and other medications that can sometimes make BSD worse.

Remember Marisol from Chapter 1? During a severe mixed episode, she developed severe hypochondriasis, which can be a form of obsessive-compulsive disorder. She called 911 six times over a period of a few weeks, sure she was dying from a rare disease. She visited countless doctors. Because she was also complaining of feeling very bad and frightened and depressed, she was prescribed high doses of antidepressants. Finally, she became so frightened and was acting so irrationally that she had to be hospitalized. At the hospital, she was given antipsychotic medication and mood stabilizers. Her hypochondriasis went away as her mood stabilized. She probably doesn't have true OCD, but she can have some symptoms when she is in a mixed state.

BSD or ADD?

People with BSD often have significant problems with memory, concentration, and attention. Many of our patients say, "My memory is like a sieve; everything just flows right through my mind." They may make endless lists or put little sticky notes everywhere with details of the things they are supposed to remember. Some may develop a fear of trying anything new, because they are so afraid they won't be able to learn the information needed.

Is this attention deficit disorder? It might be. Studies of children suggest that up to 85 percent of children with BSD have attention deficit disorder as well. This creates a significant difficulty, because the medication used to control attention deficit disorder (ADD), like Ritalin or Adderal, can sometimes make the symptoms of BSD worse. New methods are being developed to distinguish these conditions using psychological tests, but more progress is needed.

Learning disabilities are also common among individuals diagnosed with BSD. Some of the difficulties with memory and attention may be a function of a preexisting learning disability.

But many of these difficulties with memory, attention, and concentration may also be a symptom of the working memory problems frequently seen in patients with BSD. Working memory is the memory you use to process information right at the moment to help you solve problems. Working memory is necessary to hold information "online" so we can evaluate the information and use it to make appropriate decisions. Problems with working memory will make it difficult to remember new information or to quickly make decisions based on new facts. We will talk about working memory more in Chapter 4, which deals with the neurobiology of BSD. As you get more stable, some of these difficulties will decrease.

Your Diagnostic History

Think about your own diagnostic history. Did you receive other diagnoses before you received the diagnosis of BSD? Did you receive any additional diagnoses?

It can be helpful to review your medical history and list the kinds of diagnoses and treatments you have received in the past.

This can provide your doctor with some of the information he or she may need to evaluate your condition now (see Exercise 2). (By the way, if you can't remember each and every diagnosis or theory, don't be alarmed. Most people have a hard time remembering or were never told their initial diagnoses. Others can't remember their medication history. They just feel like they've taken everything.) But if you are able to fill in some of this information, it can be helpful as a guide to evaluating future symptoms and treatments.

You may also feel angry, disappointed, and sad that you have had to travel such a long and hard road to get the correct diagnosis. It is hard to be sick when doctors and scientists are in the early stages of learning about a disorder. Mistakes will be made. Incorrect diagnoses will be given, and incorrect treatments will be prescribed. The most heartbreaking mistakes come when patients get blamed for failing to get better.

Things are starting to dramatically improve, and knowledge is accumulating faster than ever before.

But you can't change history. And it is hard to accept that you may have gotten sick before scientists or doctors really had the knowledge to deal effectively with your condition.

It can be important to talk your feelings over with a therapist or friend or with another person with BSD. The patients in our BSD group spend time going over their past treatments and trying to come to terms with the misdiagnoses and well-intentioned but failed initial treatments. It is helpful to them to hear other people's stories and to know they are not alone. And it's helpful to know that substantial progress is being made every day. (Just try putting "bipolar disorder" into Google Scholar, and you will see the tremendous changes in knowledge that come every month. You may not understand all the scientific jargon, but you will be reassured by the sheer volume of the research.)

EXERCISE 2
Keeping Track of Your Medical History

Here is a sample diagnostic and medication history.

Month and Year	Doctor	Diagnosis	Treatments (medications and doses). List dose changes on a different line.	Effects of Treatment (e.g., mood changes, thinking cleared, ability to function at work, ability to get along with others)	Side Effects (e.g., tremors, weight gain, sleeping problems, sedation, agitation)
November 1990	Dr. Smith at Memorial Health Care	Depression	Prozac (20 mg a day)	Got a little less depressed	Couldn't sleep
March 1991			Prozac (20 mg a day)	Got less depressed, then I got very nervous	Nightmares, agitation
April 1991	Mt. Sinai	Bipolar depression	Hospital stay— lithium (600 mg a day), Risperdal (2 mg a day)		

Now fill in your diagnostic history and medication history.

Month and Year	Doctor	Diagnosis	Treatments (medications and doses). List dose changes on a different line.	Effects of Treatment (e.g., mood changes, thinking cleared, ability to function at work, ability to get along with others)	Side Effects (e.g., tremors, weight gain, sleeping problems, sedation, agitation)

If I'm Taking My Medication, Why Do I Feel Bad Again?

The Importance of Ongoing Assessment of Symptoms

KEY POINTS

Ongoing assessment and diagnosis are a major part of treatment.

Because BSD is a cycling disorder, the symptoms change over time.

It can be difficult to recognize your symptoms in the context of your life.

If you can recognize and correctly identify these symptoms, you can identify the nature of each new cycle.

Information about your symptoms and cycles can be used to optimize your treatment.

Fatima has been given the correct diagnosis of bipolar II. But now she is in the office complaining of being depressed and frantic with worry that she has breast cancer. She has been checking over and over to see if she has lumps. She's called her family doctor four times this week. What's going on?

Ron has bipolar I. He looks very depressed, slumped over in the chair. He can't make eye contact, and he hasn't done anything productive for days. And then he says that he has been having terrible dreams—violent dreams that seem real. Is it really depression? Or is it a mixed state? Is he still bipolar I?

Living in the Bipolar Cycle

Despite how difficult it is, getting the initial diagnosis is not enough. Because BSD is a cycling disorder, the condition changes—with the seasons, with stress, and because of other factors. You need to be able to accurately interpret the nature of these changes. Are you depressed? In a mixed state? More anxious? Hypomanic? Are you at a different point in the cycle than you were yesterday? Or are you just reacting to the normal stresses and strains of everyday life? Quickly identifying changes in symptoms and accurately interpreting their meaning is essential to obtaining the treatment you need to stabilize your mood.

Your job is to recognize changes in your symptoms and to communicate these observations or concerns to your treatment team. Then you and your team can work together to interpret these changes and to make appropriate adjustments in medication, therapy, and/or stress exposure. (And then keep monitoring to make sure you got it right.)

Sounds like a lot? It is. But it may help to think about the challenges facing people with other medical disorders, such as type I diabetes. People with diabetes have to maintain their blood sugar within a certain range. If they don't, they will suffer serious medical consequences. To ensure that their blood sugar stays within range, they need to regularly monitor their blood sugar and adjust their insulin, depending on their food intake, activity level, and other factors. They have to test their blood sugar several times a day. All this monitoring and adjusting is a big job, but with new devices, they can get pretty accurate and rapid readings.

With BSD, you have to do the same thing, except there is no meter that helps you read your symptoms or estimate your stress exposure. You have to monitor your symptoms yourself, with the help of observations from your family, friends, and treatment team. And if you see that your symptoms have changed or your stress level has increased, it may be time to make some adjustments. Maybe it's time to adjust the medication, maybe it's possible to reduce your stress, or maybe you need to get some extra support. But monitoring your symptoms and correctly interpreting their meaning is not always a straightforward task. Let's look at some of the issues to consider as you review you own symptoms.

"Is It Me or BSD?"

At any given time, it can be hard to separate symptoms of BSD from your personality characteristics, just the way you are. When you notice a change in your mood, you probably try to think about why you feel the way you do. You may think about what's happening in your life; maybe you're having a problem with another person, with money, or with your health. Most of the time, you have a great deal of information about the situation—information about the way you feel, the way you think, the circumstances you are in, and how other people act.

It can be easy to get lost in the details of your own experience. But it is still important to consider another layer of information, a clinical evaluation. The key to managing BSD effectively is to learn to look at yourself and your experiences from a clinical perspective.

What do we mean? The goal is to learn to think about whether your reactions to a particular situation also reflect changes in your underlying BSD symptoms. Specifically, you may wonder if your mood is very distressed or changeable (that is, labile) because you are upset about something specific. But it may be worth considering whether you are having a mood shift, feeling bad, and looking for an explanation for your feelings. ("I feel so upset, it must be that I hate my job.") It may be hard to tell whether a situation is causing your mood or if your mood is causing you to reinterpret the situation—but it is worth considering these issues. It can be helpful to talk these issues over with a therapist. (In Chapter 11, we will talk more about managing stressors and thinking about the ways your mood affects stress exposure and vice versa.)

When your mood changes, especially if you are depressed, the mood can reactivate your psychological "war wounds." These war wounds may include distressing thoughts or memories that are related to unresolved issues from your past. So if you feel like you were always criticized as you were growing up, when you become more depressed, you may ruminate about an episode in which you were criticized. If you were abandoned by a lover or a parent just as you were getting sick, the hurt and angry feelings you felt at the time might have been very intense. When you feel hurt again in the same way, you might reactivate the original memories. If you are very committed to achieving something in your life (for example, a successful career or great wealth) and you haven't yet succeeded, when your mood shifts, you may ruminate again and again on failure.

The particular painful circumstances of your life may not have caused BSD, but when you have BSD symptoms, you can reawaken the pain. The trick is to not get distracted using all your energy to understand why these events hurt you. First treat the symptoms and stabilize your mood. You can think things through after you have regained mood stability.

Let's look at some examples to understand how to recognize BSD symptoms in your descriptions of your thoughts, feelings, and actions.

Karina's Story

Karina had been diagnosed in her youth as ADHD. Later she was diagnosed with depression. But no matter what medication she was taking for ADHD or depression, nothing seemed to help. About six months ago, she sought out a new psychiatrist and learned she may have bipolar I. Her new psychiatrist helped her finally come out of a long period of depression in which she had been unable to work. As she was coming out of the depression, he referred her for psychotherapy.

When Karina visited my office, she wanted to talk about some issues that were occupying all her attention. She was worried that she just couldn't stop thinking about a situation with a particularly unsavory guy she had briefly dated. She found out he was dating a new girl, and she was angry and upset. She kept reviewing the situation and blaming herself—"Why didn't he like me?" "What was wrong with me?" "Why did he choose someone else?" She had the same thoughts over and over echoing in her head. She couldn't think about anything else.

She was disturbed by her thinking, and she knew it was interfering with her ability to get anything done or to socialize with her friends and family. She was afraid to interact with anyone, because if they mentioned anything about this man, she would fall into this pattern of thinking these upsetting thoughts all over again. She couldn't understand why she was so focused on a guy that she knew was bad news.

As I listened to Karina describe the situation, I was struck by how repetitive her thoughts were and how forceful the repetition was. She knew her preoccupation was irrational, but she couldn't stop the sentences from playing over and over in her mind, bouncing around inside her head. She was fully absorbed in her own thoughts: Her only focus was on her pain and herself—and whether she deserved to be treated in this manner. It was difficult to get her to think about anything else, even when she was pushed. She hadn't been able to motivate herself to do anything, and she hadn't left the house for three days.

What was going on? I separated out the content of her story (the part about the boyfriend) from the process (the way she was describing the situation and her own thoughts). She was having very high-energy thoughts. She was talking quickly, intensely, and repetitively about her concerns. The thoughts had an obsessional quality to them, and it was clear that Karina had no real control over the frequency and nature of these ideas. Her mood was very labile, or changeable. If someone mentioned this boyfriend, the obsessive thoughts would be triggered. She was exhausted and overwhelmed by her thoughts.

She had symptoms consistent with both hypomania (racing thoughts, a pressure to keep on talking, and a very high level of self-involvement, which could be a form of grandiosity) and depression (difficulty concentrating and inability to sleep), and she had a high level of interpersonal hypersensitivity and mood lability. All in all, it was worth considering a diagnosis of a mixed state.

Karina agreed, and I scheduled an emergency appointment with her psychopharmacologist. Her psychiatrist/psychopharmacologist agreed with my assessment, and he added a low dose of an anti-psychotic medication to the mood-stabilizing medication she was already taking. Once we added the antipsychotic medication to provide greater mood stabilization, she gained much greater control over her obsessional thinking.

Karina knew there were also some personal reasons why these particular thoughts might be bothering her. They reminded her of some traumatic experiences from her childhood. She realized that when her mood was bad, these psychological war wounds got reactivated.

The challenge for Karina is to avoid getting caught up ruminating over these war wounds. Although she may want to analyze the *content* of her thoughts (that is, thinking about why she chooses guys who are "bad news"), she also has to learn to look at the *quality* of her mood and thinking. For Karina, uncontrollable repetitive thoughts combined with an intensely sad mood may signal a mixed state. Once she has this mood state under control, then we can talk about "bad-news" guys, if it seems important.

Looking at the Complete Picture

Most of the difficulty in diagnosis comes from the nature of the symptoms. The symptoms of BSD seem clear when they are described in a textbook. But in real life it can be quite difficult to understand and interpret the changes in behavior and mood that are seen in BSD. The symptoms that are most obvious or cause the most pain may not be the clearest clues to your underlying condition. For example, feeling bad or upset isn't always depression. You can feel depressed when you are very anxious, or you can have symptoms of depression when you are in a mixed state. Depression, anxiety, and mixed state are treated differently, so recognizing the correct underlying condition is important.

Let's look at an example. The example highlights the importance of reviewing all your symptoms to help clarify the differences between a depressed and a mixed state.

Frank's Story

Frank has bipolar I. Recently he came to my office looking very depressed. He was slouched over and moving very slowly. He told me he felt very depressed. He couldn't stop worrying about dangerous things happening to his family. He was going to bed very late at night, and he was sleeping way too late during the day. He couldn't get started doing anything productive and was just pacing around the house. He had some suicidal thoughts.

I looked carefully at Frank. He certainly seemed as if he was in a depressive episode. But as we talked, he asked me about something that was puzzling him. He said he felt agitated, even though he knew that he looked very sluggish. Part of why he felt agitated was that all day, nonstop, advertising jingles were running through his head. He just couldn't make his brain quiet down. Over and over, he heard commercials for soda, laundry detergent, and other products.

This symptom, combined with his reports of agitation, made me rethink my diagnosis. Now I speculated that maybe we weren't looking at depression—maybe we were looking at a mixed state, in which his obvious symptoms of depression were combined with the not-as-easily discernable symptoms of mania. I called Frank's psychopharmacologist to discuss adjusting his medication. On the psychopharmacologist's advice, Frank reduced his dose of antidepressant. Within a few days, his mood brightened, and he finally stopped hearing those jingles.

As you can see, in the midst of depressive symptoms (which usually seem very straightforward), hypomanic symptoms can be hard to detect. Some patients have symptoms similar to Frank's—they have repetitive words or thoughts bouncing through their heads. Other symptoms may also indicate a mixed state. For example, when my patient Susan is in a mixed state, she looks very sluggish and depressed, but she has such vivid nightmares that the dreams seem almost real to her. Her thoughts seem to glow in color, indicating that her mind may be too activated and that symptoms of hypomania coexist with the more obvious symptoms of depression. Rachel's seemingly depressive demeanor is in sharp contrast to her more manic symptoms, which include intrusive thoughts. She sees images of her body being sliced by a very sharp sliver of glass. She clearly communicates her terror as she describes the vividness of the image. She can't stop moving or fidgeting, and her facial expressions are intense.

Using Images and Metaphors to Help with the Diagnostic Process. We often use images to help us diagnose the nature of a particular episode. Sometimes we will ask our patients if their mood is gray and sluggish (more likely to be depression) or shiny black and slippery (maybe a mixed state with a more labile mood). We have not yet tested whether these images, in fact, help correct the diagnostic and treatment process, but thinking about it in these terms does seem to have helped at least some of our patients communicate their symptoms to their psychiatrists.

It is worth noting that some neurologists working with children who suffer from headaches use the children's drawings of their pain as a way to distinguish between migraine headaches and tension headaches. The drawings of the tension headaches really look different from the ones of migraines. For example, one child with tension headaches drew a picture of his head in a vise, whereas another child with a migraine headache drew a picture of lightning striking his head.

Is it a foolproof method? No, but sometimes you can think about the pictures that come to your mind as you consider your current mood state and see if the pictures match a mixed state more than a depressed state (that is, have some energy to them rather than being altogether low energy and lifeless). It can take some time to recognize these idiosyncratic pieces of behavior as symptoms, but it can make the course of the illness more predictable and positive if you become more accurate in recognizing and describing your internal state. Talking about images and metaphors may help.

You and Your Symptoms

What do your symptoms look like? The hardest challenge for most people is to be able to step outside themselves and recognize their ideas, actions, and emotions as symptoms (when they are). It's worth doing this, even if it seems strange.

In Exercises 3 and 4, you will see a list of diagnostic symptoms and then different ways these symptoms sometimes express themselves in real life. Now that you know a little more about BSD, can you match some of your daily experiences to the symptoms listed in the diagnostic manuals? Do your symptoms express themselves differently? How did you explain these symptoms before? Did you think these feelings were depression? Anxiety? Or a response to your environment?

Were the symptoms obvious? Or were they hard to figure out? Once you are labeling your symptoms, you can monitor them more easily and communicate more effectively with your health-care providers. You can bring these exercises with you and see if your ideas make sense to the doctor. You can also ask your friends and family what they notice.

It may make you very self-conscious to try these exercises. You may want to do them with someone you trust. But once you learn how to recognize your symptoms in "real life," you will see how much more effective you are in managing BSD and how much more effective you make your treatment team.

The final exercise in this chapter is a guide to preparing for your doctor appointments. You can use it to organize the information about your symptoms that will help you and your doctor make treatment decisions. You might want to try filling it out before you go to see if it helps you make the most of the session.

EXERCISE 3
Recognizing Depressive Symptoms

Symptoms Associated with Depression (from the DSM-IV-TR, p. 356) and the Way People Commonly Describe These Experiences	The Way You Experience These Symptoms
"Depressed mood:" feeling sad, blue, numb; feeling as if you have no energy, no life, no juice	
"Markedly diminished interest or pleasure in activities:" feeling as if you have no motivation, nothing interests you, you can't get anything done because you don't feel like it	
"Significant weight loss when not dieting:" no appetite, food doesn't taste right (or significant weight gain)	
"Insomnia or hypersomnia almost every day:" unable to fall asleep or stay asleep; unable to wake up	
"Fatigue or loss of energy:" feeling exhausted all the time	
"Visible psychomotor retardation or agitation:" feeling as if you can't move or it takes so much effort to move; leaden paralysis; or needing to move, feeling as if you can't keep still	
"Feelings of worthlessness or excessive guilt:" all your memories focus on bad things; feeling as if you are bad or a loser; feeling guilty, responsible for too much; feeling as if there is no point to your life, as if you are always missing out	

Symptoms Associated with Depression (from the DSM-IV-TR, p. 356) and the Way People Commonly Describe These Experiences	The Way You Experience These Symptoms
"Diminished concentration or indecisiveness:" feeling as if your thoughts are very slow or your mind is blank; having difficulty concentrating, focusing, paying attention, keeping your mind on your work; having difficulty remembering important things or even small events during the day	
"Recurrent thoughts of death or suicide:" thinking about death, wanting to die, planning to die	

EXERCISE 4
Recognizing Manic Symptoms

Symptoms Associated with Mania (from the DSM-IV-TR, p. 362) and the Way People Commonly Describe These Experiences	*The Way You Experience These Symptoms*
"Elevated, expansive, or irritated mood:" feeling too good, an abrupt change in your mood; full of optimism; or feeling very angry, irritable, impatient, can't wait for people, think they are taking too long to do things	
"Inflated self-esteem or grandiosity:" having too much confidence, not caring what others think even when you should; having really big ideas—about being able to save the world, attract anyone, do anything; wanting much more attention, being more charismatic	
"Decreased need for sleep:" staying up later or waking earlier without feeling tired	
"More talkative than usual or pressure to keep talking:" talking more quickly than usual or talking or thinking repetitively about the same thing, unable to control the pace or content	
"Flight of ideas or subjective experience that thoughts are racing:" words or ideas jumping around in your head, chaining lots of words together because they sound interesting; sounds or jingles running through your mind	

Symptoms Associated with Mania (from the DSM-IV-TR, p. 362) and the Way People Commonly Describe These Experiences	The Way You Experience These Symptoms
"Increase in goal-directed activity or psycho-motor agitation:" too much energy—a feeling of restlessness, electric excitement; working too much, collecting too many things, traveling too much, going to too many activities	
"Distractibility:" changing the topic all the time; unable to concentrate; feeling as if you have to write everything down to remember	
"Excessive involvement in pleasurable activities that have a high potential for painful consequences:" doing things you know you should not do but feeling like you can get away with it; too much eating, drinking, drug use, spending, partying—without a sense that you can or should stop; sexual attraction to everyone or too much intense attraction to certain people; lots of sexual thoughts in your head	
Other Related Symptoms	
Mood lability: feeling as if you cannot control your mood, as if you cry one minute and are happy the next; being very sensitive; being very angry and irritable, always snapping at other people	
Heightened interpersonal sensitivity: being hyperaware of yourself; feeling as if your skin is too thin; continually focused on interpersonal contacts	

EXERCISE 5
Going to the Doctor: Using Symptom Descriptions to Communicate with Your Doctor

Here is a sample worksheet to help you prepare for a visit to the doctor.

Doctor's name: _____

Date of visit: _____

Current medications: _____

Scheduled: Yes   No   Emergency: Yes   No

Who came with you? _____

Signs and Symptoms	How Do You Feel Today?	How Have You Felt in General Since the Last Appointment?
Sleeping (difficulty falling asleep, difficulty staying asleep, waking too early, sleeping too much)	Rough night last night, difficulty falling asleep.	Generally good sleep, 11 P.M. to 9 A.M. Hardly even have problems falling asleep.
Appetite (OK, too much, too little, cravings), weight gain	Ok.	The whole past month I haven't been very hungry.
Fatigue (rate from 1 to 10; note problems in the morning)	About an 8.	Generally about a 6, still very tired.
Concentration (rate from 1 to 10; make notes about activities you can/can't do, like reading, paying bills, talking on the phone, performing tasks at work, planning activities)	6—Ok, but I can't read.	Still having trouble reading books and newspapers.

Signs and Symptoms	How Do You Feel Today?	How Have You Felt in General Since the Last Appointment?
Anxiety (rate the intensity from 1 to 10; rate the frequency: never, sometimes, often, always; note any specific circumstances)	7—I am always anxious.	I have micropanics many times a day, all month long.
Symptoms of depression (write yours in—e.g., sadness, numbness, guilt, hopelessness, repetitive thoughts—and rate them from 1 to 10)	5—I feel numb and sometimes sad.	This past month I kept thinking about my past, what hasn't gone right, why other people move forward and I don't.
Symptoms of mania (write yours in—e.g., grandiosity, excess energy, racing thoughts, too much energy, hypersexuality, irritability, risky behavior—and rate them from 1 to 10)	None.	I have no symptoms of mania.
Other symptoms (e.g., mood changeability/lability, hypersensitivity to other people)		
Thinking about suicide? Thinking about hurting others?	No. No.	A few times I thought about killing myself and about jumping in front of the train, but the thoughts passed quickly.
Side effects (e.g., sedation, weight gain/loss, sexual difficulties, mood feels funny, difficulty thinking or concentrating, rash, other)		So tired.

Signs and Symptoms	How Do You Feel Today?	How Have You Felt in General Since the Last Appointment?
Minor stressors (things that happened that were moderately difficult to deal with)		My sister came to visit for a week.
Major stressors (things that happened that were very difficult to deal with)		My husband is having work difficulty, and I am worried he will lose his job.

Other questions or concerns:

Can I take my medicine earlier so I can wake up earlier?

New instructions (medication changes or other advice):

Now here is one for you to fill in.

Doctor's name: ....

Date of visit: ....

Current medications: ....

Scheduled: Yes   No   Emergency: Yes   No

Who came with you? ....

Signs and Symptoms	How Do You Feel Today?	How Have You Felt in General Since the Last Appointment?
Sleeping (difficulty falling asleep, staying asleep, waking too early, sleeping too much)		
Appetite (OK, too much, too little, cravings), weight gain		
Fatigue (rate from 1 to 10; note problems in the morning)		
Concentration (rate from 1 to 10; make notes about activities you can/can't do, like reading, paying bills, talking on the phone, performing tasks at work, planning activities)		
Anxiety (rate the intensity from 1 to 10; rate the frequency: never, sometimes, often, always; note any specific circumstances)		

Signs and Symptoms	How Do You Feel Today?	How Have You Felt in General Since the Last Appointment?
Symptoms of depression (write yours in—e.g., sadness, numbness, guilt, hopelessness, repetitive thoughts—and rate them from 1 to 10)		
Symptoms of mania (write yours in—e.g., grandiosity, excess energy, racing thoughts, too much energy, hypersexuality, irritability, risky behavior—and rate them from 1 to 10)		
Other symptoms (e.g., mood changeability/lability, hypersensitivity to other people)		
Thinking about suicide? Thinking about hurting others?		
Side effects (e.g., sedation, weight gain/loss, sexual difficulties, mood feels funny, difficulty thinking or concentrating, rash, other)		
Minor stressors (things that happened that were moderately difficult to deal with)		

Signs and Symptoms	How Do You Feel Today?	How Have You Felt in General Since the Last Appointment?
Major stressors (things that happened that were very difficult to deal with)		
Other questions or concerns:		
New instructions (medication changes or other advice):		

What Exactly Is Going On?

Some Background on the Neurobiology of Bipolar Disorder

KEY POINTS

The research on the biological basis of bipolar disorder is growing rapidly, but there is still no complete picture of the underlying causes.

There may be different underlying causes for different aspects of the disorder.

Mood regulation depends on effective communication among different parts of the brain, including the parts responsible for complex thinking and emotion. In bipolar disorder, this communication may be impaired.

Problems in the ways brain cells communicate with each other may affect the growth of connections among new cells, affecting the functioning of certain brain areas.

Stress is a key player in mood regulation. In bipolar disorder, the effects of stress on your mood and functioning may be more problematic.

Bipolar disorder is a brain disorder. That's a scary thought. It affects a number of different functions and areas of the brain. Scientists don't understand the full story of what bipolar is (what the underlying brain dysfunctions are), but they have some ideas. Understanding these ideas can help you make better predictions about how you will recover and how stress affects you.

Why It's Good to Know

Our patients want this information. It helps them to put things in perspective and to understand the condition. In part, it fulfills their basic need to know what is happening to them. We have continually emphasized how BSD affects both mood regulation and information processing. Here we tell you the latest research on why and how. We will provide you with some background to help you understand the different brain mechanisms that might contribute to BSD. This chapter is a kind of mini Neuroscience 101 course.

The more you know, the more "clinical" you can be in approaching your own symptoms. Our experience has been that this knowledge helps people with BSD understand their symptoms more fully and recognize changes more quickly. Having greater knowledge can help you better determine when to call the doctor and when to make rapid adjustments in treatment to avoid worsening symptoms. It may help you understand more about the medications that are prescribed to you. This is all part of breaking the bipolar cycle.

But first, a cautionary note. It is also important to recognize that knowledge is growing rapidly, and some of the information in this section will be outdated (and possibly found to be incorrect) as new studies are completed. In addition, much of the information we present here reflects what scientists are learning about mood and anxiety regulation in general, not necessarily specific to BSD. The specific information is just beginning to emerge.

We have greatly simplified the presentation to try and capture the main ideas. But it is still a very complicated story. At the end of the book, we have included references to books and articles that guided this presentation and can provide you with more detail. Dr. Jim Phelps offers more detailed information, along with remarkable pictures that illustrate some of the key concepts, online at psych education.org.

A System of Connections

Your brain contains many parts. Regulating your mood depends on both the integrity of the individual parts and the integrity of the connections between them. In a way, your brain is like a city. In a city, there are sections for businesses and sections for housing and sections for leisure. To make it all work, there are roads connecting each part. Traffic signals regulate the traffic flow through each section. If the traffic signal suddenly gets stuck on red, then traffic snarls. People might be able to drive to some locations but not to others. Supplies might be able to flow to one area to fill up stores, but customers might not be able to reach those stores.

If the signal gets stuck frequently (but not permanently), and no one comes to fix it, then the system will exhaust everyone. Each time people have to drive across the street with a broken light, they have to slow down. They have to decide whether it is safe to move and then dart across, feeling a little uncomfortable the whole time. Then the next car has to make the same set of decisions—so the traffic moves in fits and starts, instead of effortlessly.

Scientists now think that bipolar disorder is at least partly a function of difficulties in the communication or signaling between brain cells, called neurons. So to take our traffic signal analogy a little further, bipolar disorder can be seen as a problem with traffic flow in the brain, and these problems are caused in part by problems with the traffic signals. But in this case the "traffic signals" are really the parts of your brain cells that help the neurons communicate with other neurons. Scientists call this a problem with cell signaling. The problems with cell signaling affect the growth and functioning of different parts of the brain. And in turn, these difficulties contribute to problems in communication between parts of the brain—communication that is essential to mood stability and many kinds of information processing.

How does this communication work? New research can give us some initial answers to these questions. The next two sections give you a summary of the research in this area. The first section includes an overview of the areas of the brain in general and then a more detailed discussion of the areas particularly relevant to BSD. Next, we are going to talk about how brain cells (called neurons) communicate and see how problems with this communication might lead to the problems in mood regulation and information processing.

The Overall Structure of the Nervous System

First, it helps to understand a little about the overall structure of the nervous system. The central nervous system (CNS) consists of the brain and the spinal cord. The peripheral nervous system (PNS) includes all the other nerves throughout our organs and the rest of our body. Both the CNS and the PNS play a role in the experience and expression of emotion. For example, our brain is involved when we think about something that makes us nervous (like taking a test). These thoughts can trigger an upset stomach, because our brain (part of the CNS) sends messages to the nerves in our gut, which are part of the PNS. Different parts of the CNS and PNS can be organized into systems. These systems are responsible for different functions, like making the coordinated movements necessary to play a game or run from danger.

A System of Emotions
To understand the biology of bipolar disorder, a mood disorder, we are interested in the systems that are responsible for emotions. It is a little problematic to think about a system for emotions (especially when it is hard to decide exactly what an emotion is!). But first let's

think more generally about what an emotion system has to do to achieve mood stability.

A number of different processes are involved in mood stability. We need to be able to recognize emotional cues (for example, the expression of anger or fear on another person's face). We also need to be able to generate appropriate emotional responses to emotional cues, which means that we have to be able to feel certain things in response to environmental cues, including other people's emotions. And we have to be able to regulate our emotional responses. Some aspects of regulation include being able to suppress the expression of emotions when appropriate, to take different perspectives on emotional situations, and to be able to shift attention flexibly from emotional to nonemotional tasks (to be able to get your mind off your feelings). And other aspects of regulation include controlling the response of your PNS as your body experiences the physical changes that go along with different emotions. The goal is to be able to use emotional cues (other people's feelings and your own) to help you more accurately and efficiently process what is going on in your environment and to help you respond more effectively to meet whatever challenges face you.

The ability to achieve mood stability and to regulate your emotions requires several different parts of your brain to coordinate effectively. Scientists still don't understand all the parts involved or how they interact, but the evidence suggests that two major areas—the limbic system and the frontal lobe (including your prefrontal cortex)—are involved.

One way to investigate the underlying difficulties in the ways people with BSD regulate their emotions is to study patterns of brain activation when people are feeling different emotions or responding to different tests that evoke emotions. For example, in some studies scientists ask people to look at pictures of other people feeling different emotions. Or scientists ask volunteers to perform tests that require attention (like math tests) as they experience different kinds of feelings. At the same time, the scientists use brain scans to identify the parts of the brain that should (or should not) be activated during these tasks. These studies, which often use fMRI (functional magnetic resonance imaging) technology, suggest that the connections between the frontal lobe and the limbic system are important to help people stay focused and effectively regulate their emotional response—that is, to recognize what they are feeling and then to use their attention effectively to be able to process the emotion and keep thinking about the tasks they are trying to accomplish.

The research is still new and all the findings do not agree, but much of the evidence suggests that part of the problems in mood regulation in BSD reflects problems in the integration of information from areas of the brain that control attention and higher-level information processing (i.e., parts of your frontal lobes and related areas) with input from the areas responsible for detecting and responding to emotional stimuli (i.e., parts of your limbic system).

Let's now look in a little more detail at how the limbic system and the frontal lobe contribute to difficulties in bipolar disorder. (See "Strategies for Studying the Brain" for a brief description of the types of studies scientists use to learn about the brain.)

Strategies for Studying the Brain

Scientists now use many strategies to try to understand the biological basis for bipolar disorder. It is amazing to realize the many different ways we can study brain structure and function.

They study the brains of individuals with bipolar versus other disorders or no disorders. Or they study people with BSD who are manic versus depressed or in a "normal" mood. They can examine brain structure and functioning using fMRI (functional magnetic resonance imaging) or PET (positron emission tomography) scans. These scans are used to get pictures of the areas of your brain that are active when you are doing different kinds of tasks that require different kinds of information-processing skills. Scientists use fMRI or PET scans to examine differences in the areas of the brain that get activated or "turn on" as the people do different tasks, especially tasks that involve memory or emotion. They can use these scans to see, for example, if certain areas of the brain are more or less active (or differ in size) in people with BSD versus "normal" controls (i.e., people without BSD or other psychiatric illnesses). Using the previous analogy, this enables scientists to more fully understand the traffic patterns in the brain. However, at this point, these tests are not used to diagnose BSD, because we just don't know what a brain with bipolar disorder looks like. But these tests are used to help us understand how the brain works in different conditions.

Researchers can also examine the postmortem (after death) brains of individuals with BSD to see if there are physical changes in the structure. They can study the brains of people who had strokes or other forms of brain damage to see how damage to a particular area of the brain affects behavior.

A new development, magnetic resonance spectroscopy (MRS), lets scientists see changes in brain chemistry. They can also use electrophysiology studies in which they put tiny little sensors into neurons (nerve cells) to measure changes in the electrical activity of the cell under different circumstances. Some of these studies are used to determine how different kinds of medications work.

Researchers can give different medications that block the actions of certain neurotransmitters or hormones (like cortisol) and see how this affects everything from cell-to-cell communication to human behavior. Many of these studies are done in animals. All these different methods have helped scientists to understand more about the functions of different parts of the brain and to determine how these parts communicate with each other to regulate functioning.

However, it is important to note that studies of the neurobiology of bipolar are still in their infancy. This is a new area of research, using new technology. The studies on people often include very small numbers of participants, and the findings are not always consistent. Many of the studies of brain activation can only tell us how one thing is associated with another. They can't yet tell us if changes in a particular brain area cause bipolar disorder. But all these studies help scientists develop better models of the neurobiology of bipolar.

The Limbic System

The limbic system is located deep in the brain and is made up of several different structures. (You might have heard of the hypothalamus, the hippocampus, and the amygdala—all parts of the limbic system.) The different parts of the limbic system communicate quickly and efficiently with each other and then relay information to and from the rest of the body and the other parts of the brain. Information flow between the limbic system and the rest of your brain and body is a two-way street.

A key part of the limbic system is the amygdala. This area is thought to act as an emotion evaluator and is sometimes referred to as a danger detector. It lets us quickly detect and respond to situations that might be dangerous. When the amygdala gets stimulated by an input signaling a threat, it sends out signals to other areas of the brain and your body indicating that it may be time for action. You may feel fear or anger as these signals are sent. (Think about what is happening when you are in a dangerous situation, such as if you are in traffic and a big truck swerves in front of you.

Your body reacts quickly. The amygdala starts a cascade of reactions throughout your body, with different hormones triggering a series of changes. The result is that your heart pounds and your hands get sweaty, among other physical changes, and you "feel" terrified.)

The Frontal Lobe

The frontal lobe has many areas within it, but the area most relevant to bipolar disorder seems to be the prefrontal cortex (PFC). As far as scientists know, this area has two major roles. One involves regulating mood. The PFC regulates emotional responses through its connections with the limbic system, particularly the amygdala. The PFC acts to slow down the action of the amygdala by sending messages to limit the signals the amygdala sends to other brain areas. This prevents the body from becoming overstressed. One theory is that in some psychiatric disorders, including anxiety disorders and possibly BSD, the PFC does not adequately slow down or regulate the actions of the amygdala. Consequently, the experience of emotion and the physical changes associated with emotion do not get regulated well.

The other job of the PFC involves information processing, including working memory and aspects of organizational thinking, sometimes called executive functioning. Working memory is the memory we use to process information right at the moment to help us solve problems. Executive functioning includes the information-processing skills we use to develop goals and make plans.

Our working memory holds information "online" to enable us to evaluate it and make appropriate decisions. Working memory isn't one process; rather, it is actually made up of several components: mental manipulation, rehearsal, short-term storage, and retrieval. For example, when you are reading this book, you may use verbal rehearsal (repeating new vocabulary words to yourself) to help you understand the concepts. Retrieval allows you to relate this new information to older information, to put it into context.

The type of thinking called executive functioning involves several different interrelated processes. Executive functioning allows you to predict outcomes or anticipate the consequences of a set of actions and to organize information or choices. These abilities are necessary to help you set goals and to figure out a reasonable course of action. Executive functioning is also involved in social behavior, helping you make social decisions and control impulses.

What does this mean for you? PFC difficulties may leave you with problems in declarative memory (difficulties learning new information). They may also lead to problems in working memory (problems working with new information and storing it effectively so you can use it to solve problems) or in initiating and planning actions. These information-processing skills are known to be impaired in BSD, and they can be among the most disabling symptoms.

The Effects of Stress

When emotion is not well regulated, you are more likely to feel stressed. Even if you don't really believe anything catastrophic has happened, poorly regulated emotions can leave you feeling as if something serious has occurred. And your body may be reacting as if it has to respond to a stressor. In addition, BSD can create more stressful life circumstances, if it interferes with your relationships or your ability to work. And because BSD tends to run in families, a more stressful environment in your childhood may also affect your ability to manage stress.

When something is identified as stressful, the hypothalamus (a ̲ of your limbic system) triggers a cascade of hormones, which ̲tually results in the release of the stress hormone cortisol. Cor-̲has effects throughout the body, increasing metabolism and ̲ging immune function.

When your body is responding to an acute threat, this is very helpful. You are getting ready to meet the increased demands. But when your body is under long-term stress and during depression, there are prolonged changes in the release of cortisol. This can lead to harmful consequences.

Cortisol can cause short-term and long-term changes in processes that are involved in neuron to neuron communication. The changes associated with too much cortisol can destroy cells in the parts of the brain that are associated with memory and other information-processing tasks. This is important to understand, because some of the symptoms associated with bipolar disorder, including depression as well as difficulties in concentration and attention and memory, may be associated with problems in the regulation of biological responses to stress, including the release of cortisol and other neurohormones.

How Cells in the Brain Communicate

What causes the difficulties in the communication between brain areas? To understand this, we need to know more about how the cells of the brain themselves communicate and how they regulate the cell-to-cell connections. These connections are essential for the proper functioning of the areas we just discussed.

You can think about the millions of nerve cells (or neurons) in your brain as communication devices. Neurons communicate with electrochemical signals. Chemicals called neurotransmitters regulate neuron-to-neuron communication. You probably have heard of many of the major neurotransmitters (for example, glutamate, norepinephrine, acetylcholine, GABA, glycine, serotonin, and dopamine).

Neurotransmitters are sent out from one neuron to another neuron. The neurotransmitters from the sending cell trigger changes in the receiving cell. These changes determine if the receiving cell will send out a message of its own and continue the chain of communication. Some neurotransmitters, like acetylcholine, are excitatory and make it more likely that the receiving cell will send on another message. Others, like GABA, are inhibitory and make it less likely the cell will send a message.

Neurotransmitters operate throughout the brain, but some also have specific areas in which they are concentrated. Each neurotransmitter has a variety of functions, and many are associated with several different pathways in the brain. For example, one of the things dopamine affects is the perception of pleasure and reward; one of the things serotonin is involved in is the regulation of sleep. Serotonin is also involved in risk-taking behavior. Changes in the way these neurotransmitters are modulated in your brain will affect the growth, development, and functioning of different areas of the brain.

How Neurons Work

A neuron, or nerve cell, is like a battery. It has extra negative (−) charges on the inside of the cell and extra positive (+) charges on the outside. Consequently, there is a difference in the electrical charge across the cell membrane. The charge difference is maintained by pumps that lie on the membrane; they keep pumping the positive charges out and keeping the negative charges in.

When a neurotransmitter is sent from one neuron to the next, it attaches to one of many little doors on the cell membrane. If the neurotransmitter is excitatory, meaning it should promote cell-to-cell communication, the neurotransmitter will make the door on the membrane open.

Neurotransmitters can "open a door" in two different ways. When the neurotransmitter attaches or binds to the membrane, it can directly open the door, letting charged particles flow back and forth. Or the neurotransmitter can bind with a receptor on the membrane and trigger a cascade of events, called a second messenger cascade, and that cascade then opens the door and lets the charged particles flow in and out. The way the door opens depends on the kind of neurotransmitter.

Once the door is open, the negative (−) charges in the cell flow out and positive (+) charges from outside the cell flow into it. This causes an electrical surge in the cell, called an action potential (AP). The AP causes the cell to release its own neurotransmitter. Cell-to-cell communication has occurred.

Studying cell signaling is a very hot new area in research on the neurobiology of bipolar disorder. What we've described here sounds pretty complex, but it's really only the tip of the iceberg. This cascade of events involves many steps along the way.

For example, some of the changes from second messenger cascades can last for seconds or up to months. The second messengers may cause immediate differences in the cell membrane that tell it, "Send a new message" or "Don't send it now." There can also be longer-lasting changes in the cell's readiness to receive messages or in the way it releases its own neurotransmitters. These second messengers can even produce changes in the way the genetic instructions located in the DNA of the cell's nucleus are carried out.

But the bottom line is that the outcome of the cascade of events influences the development of new connections among cells. One outcome of some of the second messenger cascades is to affect different chemicals, including brain-derived neurotrophic factor (BDNF) or bcl-2, that affect the development of new connections. In fact, lithium and valproic acid, two mood-stabilizing drugs, may work in part by increasing bcl-2 and promoting cell connections in certain areas of the brain.

Neurons and Memory. New research suggests that problems in certain aspects of cell signaling are specifically associated with problems in memory. When you are busy learning something or using a particular skill, for example, your brain sends nutrients to the part of your brain that is busy and facilitates cell-to-cell communication. This communication helps form new connections between cells and ensures that memory is stored properly.

You can actually see these connections in the forms of little processes or growths, referred to as dendritic spines, that grow out from the dendrites of the cell body. Depending on the type of neuron, a brain area that is responsible for something you do a lot—a busy brain area—will have lots of connections with many dendritic spines.

For example, studies in people and animals show that when they are raised in an enriched environment (with lots of social interactions and exercises and toys to play with), their brains develop many more dendritic spines connecting cells to each other. Their new and interesting experiences then create more cell-to-cell communication that further promotes the development of these spines. More connections from cell-to-cell communication probably lead to better problem-solving abilities.

When there are interruptions in cell communication, the experiences you have can't be stored in the same way, because the connections from cell to cell cannot form properly. Similarly, during periods of high stress, stress hormones (like cortisol and norepinephrine) bind or attach to the cell membrane and influence the second messenger cascades, so they either can't send the proper message to the next cell or don't send a message at all. In fact, studies have shown that stress hormones inhibit the growth of these connections, and severe chronic stress contributes to the destruction of cells in the hippocampus (an area involved in memory) and possibly the PFC. This is a direct way that stress has an effect on the symptoms of BSD. (By the way, this doesn't mean you should avoid all stress, only that you need to learn how to recognize and manage it well. More on this in Chapter 11.)

Some of the results of these biological changes affect the parts of the brain that are involved in mood and behavior. When communication is not working as it should, it may be harder for the brain areas that regulate emotional states to function. And when there are changes in the excitability of the cells, this can influence the communication of information about emotions or the regulation of emotional experiences—making us more depressed or more impulsive.

Much more research is needed to understand the processes involved in cell signaling and to examine the ways cell signaling affects the development and functioning of different brain areas. And scientists still need to understand how these biological processes affect behavior and mood. But they are on their way to developing reasonable models that will help us understand the biological basis of BSD.

Your Brain and Other Symptoms of BSD

Let's talk about your other symptoms and how they fit into an understanding of the way your brain works.

Cycles of Energy, Appetite, and Sleep

BSD is also associated with problems related to circadian rhythms. Circadian rhythms are daily rhythms that coordinate our periods of waking and sleeping, eating, daily changes in our body temperature and energy, and other cycling changes. The hypothalamus regulates rhythms of eating and sleeping and energy. This can have a big effect on whether you feel good. For example, if the timing of circadian rhythms is off, some clocks (like the internal temperature clock) may be out of sync with our night and day clock. These disruptions in circadian rhythms can interfere with sleep and with waking comfort. You can end up feeling jet-lagged, even if you have never been on a plane.

Circadian rhythms also influence the second messenger cascades, affecting cell signaling. Some treatments for BSD, like Social Rhythm Therapy, try to control the symptoms of BSD by strictly regulating the timing of different activities in an attempt to readjust circadian rhythms. The mood-stabilizing medication lithium also seems to help regulate circadian cycles.

Light and Mood
Problems in the underlying biology of circadian rhythms may explain part of the reason there are often seasonal changes in your mood and other symptoms. Different seasons are associated with different amounts of sunlight during the day, and the sunlight shines on the earth at different angles at different times of the year.

Cells from the retina in the eye go directly to the part of the brain—the suprachiasmatic nucleus of the hypothalamus, to be exact—that directs at least part of our circadian rhythms. So changes in the way sunlight hits the retina can produce changes in mood and arousal. Although this occurs in everybody, these changes in mood or arousal caused by changes of light and changes in the circadian rhythms can be particularly difficult or pronounced for people with BSD.

Sex Hormones and the Brain
Many women notice that their mood problems get worse around certain times of the month, particularly just before they get their period. One reason may be that some sex hormones, especially cer-

tain kinds of progesterone, affect cell communication. More specifically, sex hormones can affect the way the membrane responds to neurotransmitters or can affect the release of neurotransmitters, thereby influencing cell-to-cell communication.

Sex hormones can also cause longer-term changes in the ways genes in the cell are expressed (that is, change the way the genes provide instructions to create new proteins). In turn, this can change the excitability of the cell over the longer run.

Neurobiology and Your Medications

Understanding these cell-signaling pathways also helps us understand the medications for bipolar disorder. It is important to recognize that bipolar is probably not a function of a single neurotransmitter system. For example, it's not just a serotonin problem. Instead, it may be a problem in the systems that regulate the release of these neurotransmitters, including the second messenger systems. It may be the case that these problems occur more often in cells that are involved in serotonin and dopamine pathways in the brain, but other pathways also seem to be involved.

The Effect of Medications on Your Brain

The medications we take for BSD work on different aspects of BSD, but on some level they all work on the cell signaling just described. For example, there is good evidence now that lithium and some of the new mood-stabilizing medications affect these second messenger cascades, which are the biochemical pathways in the cell that can move the chemical and electrical messages through the cell. Changing these cascades affects the way the cell communicates with other cells and the growth of new connections among cells. These medications may also affect the actions of different neurotransmitters, like serotonin and dopamine.

Many antianxiety medications attach to the cell membranes and help inhibit cell communication. Antidepressants work by increasing the amount of neurotransmitters, like dopamine or serotonin, available for cell-to-cell communication. The different antidepressants do this in different ways, changing the sending cell to prevent it from reabsorbing the neurotransmitters and changing the receptors on the receiving cell to influence the way the neurotransmitters affect communication. And they seem to change the growth factors in the brain as well.

In contrast, most of the antipsychotic medications, like Haldol, Abilify, or Seroquel, block dopamine receptors, inhibiting certain kinds of cell-to-cell communication. This is a very simplified version of the story. More details are available from the resource materials we have listed at the end of the book.

Do I Have to Take My Meds?

The Role of Medications in Managing BSD

KEY POINTS

BSD has many symptoms.

The symptoms can look like one problem but really be another.

There are a variety of different medications to help manage many of these symptoms.

Medications for one problem can make other symptoms worse.

Close medical supervision is the key. It is important to keep in close touch with your doctor and to work closely to evaluate the benefits and consequences of medication.

There is no perfect solution.

BSD is a medical disorder, and medicines are generally required for effective treatment. Many people with BSD are treated very effectively with a single mood-stabilizing medication, like lithium. They have significant symptom reduction and few side effects. But for many others, finding the right medications is not always easy.

As we have seen, the most serious difficulty is getting the right diagnosis. It can be difficult for both clinicians and patients to recognize symptoms of bipolar disorder and to identify the underlying disorder contributing to the development of the symptoms. Sometimes changes in mood and behavior are just part of life—a transitory reaction to the stresses and strains of everyday experiences. Other times new symptoms can be a reflection of underlying changes in mood. The symptoms of BSD change over time and with different circumstances. Consequently, some people may need medication changes, sometimes several times a year.

"Can't I Just Pop a Few Pills?"

So you can't just get a diagnosis and a few pills and forget about BSD. BSD is a complex and fluctuating disorder. And therefore the treatment of BSD is complex and requires persistent and careful monitoring. You will need to take an active part in your own treatment team. You will learn to think like a clinician, like a doctor.

Getting the right kind of treatment can be extremely frustrating, but it is necessary to keep trying. Remember that bipolar disorder is a life-threatening condition. About half of all patients with BSD will make a suicide attempt, and somewhere between 11 and 15 percent will succeed. You can't just get over it. And most of the time, you will require medications to control your symptoms.

In the early days of psychopharmacology (the 1950s and '60s), the treatments for BSD were generally pretty limited. Very few medications were available: some sedating antipsychotics (remember Thorazine?) and lithium. These medications helped with some symptoms, but they didn't treat others. Because they had so few options, when their patients' symptoms persisted, doctors tried higher doses of the existing medications. And patients spent a lot more time in the hospital; some even spent most of their lives in psychiatric wards.

Especially at high doses, these early medications had substantial side effects. They flattened out patients' emotions, put them at risk for gaining a lot of weight, and made them feel and look tired and lethargic, or zombielike. But most important, they just didn't do the full job. BSDs can require more complex medical treatment, and the few medications available in the early stages of treatment just couldn't treat the wide range of symptoms that patients have. So although many patients got somewhat better, most still had pretty severe limitations in functioning.

For many patients, the side effects (or the worries about the side effects) outweighed the benefits. And many people who were sick (but not yet treated) felt pretty scared. They were scared to be diagnosed, because they were scared that someone would put them in the hospital or force them to take high doses of these medications. Because the medications can make a pretty big difference in some aspects of human suffering (even when they are not used efficiently), other people (for example, doctors or family members) would sometimes try to force patients to try these medications. These other people weren't necessarily being cruel, but there were so few options available that even a bad choice might have seemed better than nothing.

With stories about these kinds of experiences and the visible side effects of the early psychiatric medication regimens, a tough disorder got scarier and more stigmatizing to some people. And the medications seemed even more mysterious and dangerous.

But the situation has changed. We know enough about the kinds of medications needed and how they work that you don't have to succumb to fear. You can learn about BSD and the treatments and side effects, and you can talk things over with your doctor. The medications are still scary, but you can really learn a lot about your condition and your treatment options, which will help you make informed decisions about the best course of action for you.

The Role of Medications in BSD

Studies have shown that patients with BSD are taking an average of four and a half different medications, which means some are taking fewer but many are taking more medication.

Why so many medications? Bipolar disorder has a number of different symptoms, reflecting difficulties in several different areas or systems of the brain (as we outlined in the last chapter). You may need medicines to help stabilize your mood, curb your manic or hypomanic symptoms, relieve your depressive symptoms, manage your anxiety, control psychoses, improve your information processing, and compensate for side effects produced by other medications. Wow.

Ideally, you would like to have one medication that treats a broad range of existing symptoms. Some mood stabilizers, including lithium, can address many of these symptoms, with the beneficial effects actually increasing over time. But sometimes you need more than one medication to stabilize mood or control the other symptoms, because the different medications may help by working through slightly different pharmacological pathways. And sometimes you have persistent symptoms that just don't resolve with a mood stabilizer alone. Despite the huge increase in research, researchers and doctors just don't have perfect solutions or even a perfect understanding of what is wrong. But progress is being made every day.

The Big Picture on Medications

What's the bottom line? The medications can make a tremendous difference in your ability to function, to feel OK, and to want to stay alive. They can move bipolar disorder from being a life-threatening illness to being a chronic condition. A tough condition but manageable. This is the kind of progress that has been made for diabetes and other serious illnesses. It is starting to happen for bipolar disorder, too.

But it is still very much a work in progress. You, your doctor, and the people close to you are collaborators—observing symptoms, stressors, supports, and side effects. It's an ongoing conversation. With knowledge about your condition, you can help improve the quality of your medical care.

You may have to make many different medication changes to get a reasonable set of medicines that work for you. (And then you may have to change the medicines again as your symptoms change.) It can be exhausting and dispiriting to go through the effort of trying different medications and then switching if they don't work or if they cause too many side effects. But unless you are very lucky and your doctor gets it right on the first try, this is the only way to make progress. That's why it's necessary that you have a close relationship with a therapist or doctor or friend—to help you keep perspective during the ups and downs of the process of recovery.

Going It Alone

Many people, at some point, decide to go off medication and try to fight the disorder using their willpower alone. Sometimes dealing with the side effects of some of the medications becomes too overwhelming. Sometimes it's hard to believe that you can't make these symptoms go away if you just try harder. And sometimes people feel so much better that they want a chance to see if they can keep up the improvements without the medications. Some people go through this "on meds, off meds" cycle several times. This seems to be part of the process of accepting what needs to be done. If you need to try this path, it is safer and wiser to work closely with your doctor and your family to make sure you have support and monitoring during this period.

One issue worth considering is that if you do go off your medications or don't want to start medications, you increase the risk of relapse (having new episodes of illness). New episodes make further episodes somewhat more likely. And it can get harder to treat each new episode. It can feel like taking the medications is a big risk, but not taking them is risky as well.

"Which Medication Is for Me?"

How does your doctor know what medications to give you? Your doctor will make a judgment based on a systematic (but also intuitive) evaluation of your condition. Your doctor thinks about your symptom reports and history as well as his or her observations, knowledge of the disorder, and past experience with patients. The doctor may consult with other professionals to see if they have had patients with similar problems. But the judgment is still an educated guess, because there are no tests at present to determine what the symptoms mean or which medication is right for you. (At some point in the not-too-distant future, doctors will be able to use your DNA or other information to make better predictions about what medications will work.)

When we say "guess," we mean no disrespect to the prescribing physicians. We use the word *guess* to highlight the need for you to be a systematic and effective partner in the process of arriving at that judgment and to remind you that treatment is an interactive process. Your doctor makes a decision, and you give feedback to help figure out if you are on the right track or not. There is no way to guarantee beforehand that the decision is correct.

This doesn't mean you are a guinea pig or that the doctor doesn't know what he or she is doing. It means that the situation is complicated, because similar symptoms can emerge from different under-lying conditions. It can be hard to figure out whether a particular set of symptoms really is depression (and therefore should be treated with antidepressants) or if it is a mixed state. Co-occurring disor-ders, like anxiety or attentional disorders, can confuse the picture and make prescribing more difficult.

Keep in mind that the prescribing doctor needs all the pieces of the puzzle. Remember Frank from Chapter 3? He wouldn't have thought to complain about having those songs in his head. He thought of it as an annoying experience, not as a symptom. I kept asking questions, because not all the symptoms seemed to fit together. And the information Frank provided helped guide his psychiatrist.

But doctors won't always keep probing. It can help if you try to describe the quality of your thoughts. Are they fast or slow? Are you making connections between ideas quickly or slowly? Do your thoughts and feelings seem to bounce around or follow a straight path? Do your ideas seem to glisten and fill you with feelings? Do you feel as if you have no thoughts, as if your mind is blank or empty? Descriptions like this can really help your doctor figure out what is going on.

How do you decide what medication is right for you? Ultimately you and your doctor take an empirical approach. That means you start with observations about your symptoms, and you try a medi-cation strategy. You and your doctor will carefully monitor your symptoms and track your side effects. Together you weigh the costs and benefits, both before and after you start the course of treat-ment. No medicine is perfect. But together with your doctor, you can evaluate the risk-benefit ratio.

In the next sections, we will review the different classes of medi-cations you may be prescribed and explain some of the reasons why you might be given a certain medication. We can give you some tips on what to look out for and how to talk to your doctor and family about these issues.

It is important to note that we are not physicians. We are psychologists, and we work very closely with psychopharmacologists. In this chapter, we mean to provide a general overview of some of the medications you might be on. At the end of this book, we have included more resources in the reference section. We don't list every possible side effect. Instead, we just highlight the most common kinds of side effects. The goal is to help give you a general guideline for evaluating the trade-offs—the decisions each person must make about the costs and benefits of each medication. Your best bet is to discuss the pros and cons of each medication with your doctor.

A general note about side effects: it is important to remember that some medications have rare, but potentially serious or fatal, side effects (for example, neuroleptic malignant syndrome with antipsychotics, serotonergic syndrome with antidepressants, and Stevens-Johnson syndrome with Lamictal and some other medications). These rare but serious side effects don't mean that you shouldn't take the medications. They mean that you should be aware of the warning signs, so you can get immediate treatment if you show symptoms of these disorders.

Let's look now at the issues involved with each category of medication.

Mood-Stabilizing Medications

Mood-regulation problems are a core feature of BSD. Most people with BSD will be taking one or more mood-stabilizing medications. These can include lithium (Eskalith, or lithium carbonate) or some of the newer medications, such as Depakote (sodium valproate or divalproex sodium), Lamictal (lamotrigine), Neurontin (gabapentin), Keppra (levetiracetam), Zonegran (zonisamide), Gabatril (tiagabine), Tegretol (carbamazepine), and Topamax (topiramate). These medications are usually the frontline treatment for bipolar.

The Trade-Offs. Mood-stabilizing medications can be very effective for mood stabilization, and lithium is still often the best choice. A good response to lithium is actually a good sign for the course of the disorder. But not every mood stabilizer helps every patient. That is why it is important to take an empirical approach. If one doesn't work, after an adequate trial at the proper dose, don't give up. Keep a record and try another one because chances are very good that one or more of these medications will help. Some, like Neurontin and Topamax, can help with anxiety. Lamictal can help lift your mood, because it has some antidepressant properties. As we discussed in Chapter 4, there is new evidence that some of these medications can also help underlying brain functioning. Usually, if you can't tolerate the side effects of one of these medications, you can try another.

On the other hand, all these medications can make you feel tired. You may feel as if it takes you too long to find words (although that can also be an information-processing symptom of bipolar disorder itself). Most but not all of the medications in this class are associated with weight gain, and several cause tremors. With lithium and Depakote (and sometimes Lamictal) doctors will ask you to get blood tests to check your blood levels of the medication. At higher doses, people can feel too flat or not like themselves. Sometimes doctors will try two or more mood-stabilizing medications at the same time so they can use lower doses of each one.

Sometimes people can be very scared to take lithium, because they associate it with "being crazy" or they remember people talking about being a zombie on lithium. If your doctor thinks you should try lithium, talk about your fears. You can ask if it is safe to go slowly, starting with small doses and working your way up. This will help you understand the costs and benefits. It is worth remembering that the benefits can be substantial. Because lithium is an older medication, doctors have a lot more experience with and knowledge about it.

Antipsychotic Medications

These medications are called antipsychotics or atypical antipsychotics, but they really have many other functions. In fact, there are proposals to change the category name of antipsychotics because they work on so many different kinds of symptoms. Many patients take medications in this category to help curb manic symptoms, to treat pervasive anxiety, and to control psychotic symptoms, like hallucinations. Examples of some of the older (but often still very effective) medications include Trilafon (perphenazine), Orap (pimozide), and Haldol (haloperidol). The newer medications, called atypical antipsychotics, include Zyprexa (olanzapine), Risperdal (risperidone), Abilify (aripiprazole), Seroquel (quetiapine), and Geodon (ziprasidone). Another relatively new medication is Clozaril (clozapine). Some of these medications, like Seroquel, are also indicated to treat depression in bipolar disorder.

You may wonder why you are asked to try a medication that was originally developed for treating other mental illnesses, including schizophrenia. You may wonder if your doctor suddenly thinks you have some other illness or that other people will wonder if they find out you are taking these medications. But, in fact, many of these medications are approved for treating symptoms of BSD, and they are used more commonly than you might suspect.

The Trade-Offs. Antipsychotic medications can be tremendously effective in stabilizing your mood. They can significantly reduce the very disabling anxiety that accompanies BSD. In fact, even though they are known for being sedating, if you are exhausted by anxiety, these medications can actually give you more energy as they treat the anxiety. It is important to emphasize the powerful and positive symptom-reducing effects of these medications, when they are used correctly under close supervision.

All these antipsychotic medications can certainly make you more tired and put you at risk for muscle stiffness, and most can cause weight gain and make you feel slowed down. They can give you muscle or movement side effects called Parkinsonism or extra-pyramidal symptoms, including tremors or muscle stiffness. If you are having problems with this type of side effect, you can get another medication to treat the side effects or you can switch to another anti-psychotic medication or another class of medications.

One of the side effects is called akisthesia—feelings of restless-ness and agitation where you want to jump out of your skin. (This is a rare but extremely unpleasant side effect.) When you complain about akisthesia, you can sound like you are complaining about feel-ings of anxiety or agitation. And this can make your doctor increase the medication rather than stop it. When you talk to your doctor, it's important to raise the possibility that you might be suffering from akisthesia and to really try to accurately describe your symp-toms as best you can.

Here is the primary difficulty: as is the case with all the catego-ries of medication prescribed for bipolar disorder, these medications require close medical supervision. For these antipsychotic medica-tions in particular, you must monitor your weight. Your doctor will check your blood glucose levels to check for diabetes and will moni-tor your liver enzymes and other functions.

The bad side effects that are sometimes reported in the newspaper (such as tremendous weight gain) may be avoidable to some degree, if you and your doctor are carefully monitoring your response to the medication. To get effective symptom control, you may end up having to tolerate some weight gain. But major weight gain doesn't happen overnight, although it can happen over a period of weeks to months. If you are gaining too much weight, you may need help monitoring your diet. Or you may need to try another medication.

Recent evidence suggests that part of the reason you gain weight on some of these medications is because of the effects of the drugs on chemicals like leptin, a hormone that signals that you are full. Research on the effects of these medications on hormones and metabolism will help scientists develop new treatments in the future that have fewer side effects (or at least medications to help control the side effects).

Antidepressants

As we have seen in previous chapters, depression or depression-like symptoms are a common and debilitating feature in BSD. This depression needs to be treated carefully. There are twenty-three different antidepressants currently available, including tricyclic antidepressants such as Norpramin (desipramine), Elavil (amitriptyline), or Tofranil (imipramine); monoamine oxidase inhibitors (MAOIs) such as Parnate (tranylcypromine) or Nardil (phenelzine) or the new Deprenyl (selegline); and selective serotonin reuptake inhibitors (SSRIs) such as Prozac (fluoxetine), Zoloft (sertraline), Paxil (paroxetine), Celexa (citalopram), Luvox (fluvoxamine), or Lexapro (escitalopram). There are also "double-action drugs" such as Effexor (venlafaxine HLC) that work through several pathways. And there are medications like Wellbutrin (bupropion) that fall into their own category.

The Trade-Offs. Antidepressants can lift your mood, improve your concentration, decrease your obsessions, and reduce your anxiety.

They are commonly prescribed medications, but they can sometimes make things worse for people with BSD. And the evidence for using antidepressants in bipolar depression is mixed. Antidepressants can sometimes trigger hypomania or mixed state. In fact, one form of BSD, bipolar III, is diagnosed when individuals show symptoms of BSD only after they were treated with antidepressants or other stimulating medicines. Antidepressants can increase the excitability of the nerve cells and increase cell-to-cell communication. In some cases, this makes the symptoms worse. But other times that's just what does the trick and lifts the negative mood.

How can you know if you should try antidepressants for your depressive symptoms? You won't know for sure, but you can begin to make an educated decision after you consider issues such as those discussed in the following.

■ **Were you originally treated with antidepressants?** Many patients (as many as 50 or 60 percent) were originally diagnosed with major depressive disorder (MDD). They were often prescribed antidepressants, sometimes for years, before they were correctly diagnosed. In some cases, it is possible that antidepressant use precipitated the manic episode.

If you were treated with antidepressants before, did your symptoms get better or worse or did the effectiveness change over time? You might have felt better initially and then six to twelve weeks later thought, "The antidepressant stopped working." It might not be that the antidepressant stopped "working." Instead, it might be wise to consider if you were starting to develop symptoms of a mixed or hypomanic state and that the antidepressant was either not helping or actually making matters worse.

How can you tell if you are "switching" to a hypomanic state? When you took the antidepressant, did you get a lift in energy that helped you function or did you get electric high-intensity energy? Did you feel more intensely sad? Have more vivid nightmares? Feel your thoughts race a little more, get more irritable or impatient, have too many ideas, or feel too close to or too passionate about other people? Did other people think you sounded intense, as if your voice was vibrating with energy? Did you have an increase in suicidal thoughts? Did you feel as if you were rotting or rotten? Did you feel as if you were "tripping," or hallucinating, even after a short trial? If you think you got more intense on the antidepressants, then maybe you had moved into a mixed or hypomanic state. Again, here is where accurately defining and describing your symptoms to a loved one or health-care professional can be so very important.

However, it is important to note that your friends and family may be more accurate than you are in describing the changes you undergo. The positive or intense mood you feel during hypomania can make it really difficult for you to be objective about your symptoms. In our group for BSD, patients have made it clear that they don't necessarily experience the same symptoms on the inside as are apparent to everyone else on the outside. For example, as one group member said, "What looks like racing thoughts and grandiosity to other people feels like extra creativity and confidence to me." You also might have had the same experience of being "unaware" of your own behavior.

If you became hypomanic or edgy on antidepressants before, you may have these symptoms more quickly if you try them again. (On the other hand, sometimes you won't have problems on a new antidepressant.) So if you got into a hypomanic or mixed state after six weeks on the antidepressant the last time, you may move into that state in a much shorter time now. If you are having these symptoms, then you should call your doctor.

■ **Did other people in your family do better or worse on anti-depressants?** New evidence suggests that there are some underlying biological or genetic factors that may make some people more susceptible to "flipping" or "switching" mood states with antidepressants. However, doctors don't know what these genes are, and they don't yet have a test for the genes. But you can still get an idea if you ask questions. If other people in your family have taken antidepressants, you can ask them how the medications worked for them. Did they do better or worse? Did they have nightmares once they started, or did their sleep improve? Did they feel as if they had more intense symptoms after a while or less intense? Did they start drinking alcohol more? Did they get very restless? Did they get more suicidal?

The possibility that antidepressants may trigger a mixed or hypomanic episode doesn't mean they can never be used in BSD depression. In fact, they can be very helpful, and some (but not all) of our patients use antidepressants regularly. The psychiatrists we work with generally consider antidepressants primarily when patients are also being treated with mood-stabilizing or antipsychotic medication, and good trials of these medications have failed to relieve distress. They are thoughtful in their use of antidepressants, because they can increase symptoms. So you and your doctor need to monitor your response carefully. It just won't be enough to get a prescription and a visit in a month's time. It is important to track your progress and maybe ask someone close to you to help as well, and then you must make sure you can check in with your doctor regularly.

You will be better able to evaluate your progress and the effects of the medication if you are reasonably systematic about evaluating your symptoms. It can be very hard to think about your symptoms when you are in a low or distressed mood. Your mood at the time you are thinking about your situation often will overwhelm your ability to recall a more detailed history. You may think, "I feel terrible now—I always felt terrible, just overwhelmed." It probably isn't true that you have always felt terrible, even if you feel very bad right now. Exercise 6 (at the end of the chapter) will help you keep track of changes in symptoms when you take medication to treat depression.

Other Possibilities. Antidepressants are not the only solution for symptoms that look like depression. You can feel as if you are depressed, but you may really be in a mixed state. Your symptoms might include more changeable (or labile) moods and a hypersensitivity to other people or bad news. You might be having more nightmares.

Sometimes mood-stabilizing medications (including lithium) or antiepilepsy medications (such as Depakote, Neurontin, Lamictal, or Zonegran) can be helpful. These medications can change the level of your mood and also stabilize it. The effects might not occur right away, but they will often be seen over a relatively short period.

Sometimes people get depressed because they are so sick of being very anxious. As we have discussed, anxiety disorders and an anxious personality are common in people with BSD. There is also some new evidence that increases in hypomania or mania can increase anxiety, which in turn can lead to depression, adding fuel to the fire.

Often people can be very anxious without necessarily identifying it as anxiety. But they may be aware that they are worrying a lot or are internally preoccupied with concerns or feel as if they just cannot tolerate any more stress. They may just feel very tense and unwilling to take any action. In these cases, what looks like depression may really be intense paralyzing anxiety. This anxiety can sometimes be helped by other types of medications, including the antipsychotic medications. These medications can sometimes relieve symptoms that look like this kind of depression, because they are very effective in treating major anxiety.

However, just to make it more complicated, there are also times when these medications worsen depression and can make you feel more tired. No wonder you have to keep careful track of your symptoms and the side effects!

Antianxiety Medications

Anxiety is a major problem in BSD. Many patients report having micropanics (that is, mini panic attacks). Others report feeling overwhelmed with a destabilizing anxiety all the time, so much so that they don't really recognize it as anxiety—it is just a sense of not feeling right in their chest or gut. There are many different medication strategies to use. Sometimes the antipsychotic medications described earlier are the right answer.

Antidepressants are a frontline medication for anxiety, but as we have discussed, they have special problems in BSD. Very commonly, doctors use benzodiazepines—for example, Valium (diazepam), Librium (chlordiazepoxide), Xanax (alprazolam), Ativan (lorazepam), and Klonipin (clonazepam)—to treat anxiety in patients with BSD. Buspar (buspirone) is an atypical antianxiety medication.

The Trade-Offs. Antianxiety medications can be very helpful in reducing acute symptoms of anxiety. The side effects depend on the medication you are prescribed. For example, benzodiazepines are very effective, but they can have some long-term effects on cognitive functioning, they can be addictive, and they are sedating. (That's why you often take these medications at night to help you sleep.)

These medications require monitoring to make sure that you are not inappropriately increasing your dose or getting too sedated.

Medications to Facilitate Information Processing

Information-processing problems are a major issue for people with BSD. Some physicians will prescribe medications used to treat attention deficit disorder, including stimulants like Ritalin, Focalin, or Concerta (formulations of methylphenidate) or Adderal or Dexedrine (formulations of dextroamphetamine). They may also use medications like Provigil (modafinil) or Strattera (atomoxetine) to help.

Sometimes patients are offered medications that were developed for Alzheimer's disease, like Namenda (memantine) or Aricept (donepezil). These medications help prevent the breakdown of acetylcholine in the brain. Acetylcholine is a neurotransmitter that is important for learning and memory.

The Trade-Offs. Stimulant medications work very quickly, and they can improve cognitive function, including the ability to pay attention and concentrate for longer periods. Most decrease fatigue and can help offset sedation.

But stimulant medications may make you feel jittery or anxious. More important, these medications can increase the risk of switching to hypomania or even precipitate psychosis. That doesn't mean you shouldn't try these medications—it means that if you try them, do so with supervision and be aware that if your mood shifts, you may need to stop the medication and take another medication to help restore your mood regulation.

Medications developed for Alzheimer's disease take longer to work, but some people find them helpful (though very expensive). There are a variety of generally mild side effects, like tiredness or anxiety, dizziness or stomach distress. You may need to monitor your concentration and functioning over a few months to decide if these medications are making a difference and make sense for you.

Thyroid Hormones

Many patients with BSD take thyroid hormones, usually Synthroid or Cytomel. These medications compensate for changes in thyroid functioning that are probably caused by lithium, and they are also used to facilitate antidepressant effects. There is some evidence that people with BSD may be more at risk for thyroid abnormalities.

The Trade-Offs. These drugs can be both necessary and helpful, though too much can cause jitteriness and agitation and too little can be associated with fatigue and body aches. You will need to work closely with your doctor to monitor these medications, usually by getting regular blood tests.

Describing Your Symptoms

At the risk of repeating ourselves: the more you know about how to think about and organize your symptoms, the better you can communicate with your doctor. The better the communication, the more likely you will find the right treatment.

Your reports are essential for making the treatment work. Over time, you will learn to more quickly recognize symptoms and put together your constellation of symptoms and different diagnoses.

Following is an example that illustrates how you and your doctors can collaborate, even when it isn't clear what the best course of action should be. And after that is a story that illustrates what happens when you get really good at recognizing your symptoms and communicating with your treatment team.

Samantha's Story

Samantha has a long history of bipolar disorder II. She has had episodes of mixed state with symptoms including intense irritability, accompanied by longer and more pronounced episodes of depression.

Last year Samantha was taking a combination of two mood stabilizers. She was making good progress in recognizing and controlling her symptoms, particularly her hypersensitivity to interpersonal slights. Toward the middle of the summer, her last freelance job ended. Although she was worried about money, she decided the time was right to have a surgical procedure (completely unrelated to BSD) that she had been postponing.

The surgery went well, but it left her very sore. She had some postsurgical difficulties, which made her anxious. A few days after the operation was over (but when she still felt unwell), she started to feel very panicked, confused, and unhappy. Her psychiatrist prescribed a benzodiazepine as an antianxiety medicine. The medication helped a little, but the symptoms persisted. Samantha began to have bad dreams. She felt as if she were losing control. She cried frequently and didn't feel like she could resume her normal life.

Was she in a state of agitated depression? That was a possibility. She had been depressed before, and the surgery could have served as a stressor triggering a depression. She had tried antidepressants before with some positive benefits. Hoping to relieve some of her distress following surgery, Samantha's psychiatrist gave her a low dose of an antidepressant she had been treated with before.

Within a few days she was clearly worse. The intensity of her negative mood increased, and she felt completely disorganized. She couldn't write clearly and felt very, very anxious. Her nightmares intensified and felt like they were "breaking through" into her waking hours.

We decided that Samantha's symptoms probably indicated a mixed state, not an agitated depression. Her psychiatrist stopped the antidepressant and started Samantha on a low dose of an antipsychotic instead. In two days Samantha was feeling much better and was able to function at a much higher level, participating in her own care.

Samantha's Solution. Finding the right combination of drugs after her surgery was a very difficult process for both Samantha and her doctors, and at times Samantha felt frantic and miserable. She was very frightened by how strange, unpredictable, and intense her symptoms seemed. But the trial-and-error process worked for her, and she recognized this. She remembers this time in her life as one of the most scary times she has ever been through. And yet she says she thinks she is doing better now than she would have been if it had never happened.

Samantha knew how to make her concerns known to us, and she knew that we would change the course of treatment until we found a solution. Now she feels much, much better on the current medication program. (And she is back at work.)

How We Worked Together to Stabilize Samantha's Mood. Let's look at the process in a little more detail. First, and most important, Samantha called when she didn't feel well. Her treatment team (the psychologist and psychiatrist) talked on the phone and discussed her symptoms. She certainly was anxious (and who wouldn't be after the surgery?), but it wasn't the only problem. She had other symptoms that made it difficult to know whether she was depressed or in a mixed state. We made an educated guess but let her know that the treatment might not work. We instructed her to keep tabs on her symptoms (for example, her sleep, thinking, energy, and anxiety).

And when the first medication choices made the situation worse, Samantha knew to call back.

We scheduled appointments soon after the surgery and the first medication changes. Each time we made a medication change, we gave Samantha instructions to call us in one or two days, depending on her condition. Samantha knew she might feel worse from the treatment, but she was prepared, and she did not feel alone. Because we kept in close contact, we didn't have to be magicians and "guess" right the first time. In fact, we made a total of four medication changes over about a month. It would have been better to get it right the first time, but that isn't always possible. At every step of the way, Samantha was part of the decision-making process.

Henry's Story

Henry is a sixty-five-year-old man who had a major manic episode five years ago. Over the past year, his mood has generally been more stable, with a lingering mild depression. Recently, Henry came to an appointment and reported that he was worried he might be getting a little hypomanic. He looked about the same as usual, maybe a little more alert. But he told me he felt like his speech was pressured (and it was). He was emphasizing his words, speaking more rapidly, and sounding rushed (even though we were really not in a hurry). He was feeling a little hypersexual, having a lot of intrusive thoughts about sex.

He wondered if he should try stopping the small dose of antidepressant he had been taking for his lingering depressive symptoms. The psychiatrist and I agreed that this might be the most conservative and easiest approach. We asked him to keep us posted on any changes. Henry stopped the antidepressant, and within about five days, he called back to say that this strategy didn't work. His hypersexuality decreased slightly, but he was now so depressed he could not get out of bed or go to work. He had more thoughts about killing himself, but fortunately he didn't have a plan or an intent. The psychiatrist decided she would treat the hypomania more directly and added back the antidepressant and increased his dosage of lithium by a third. Within a few days, his mood was stable again, and he was back at work. He barely had time to sink into the hopeless thinking (for example, "I will never get better. This condition will ruin my life.") that had been characteristic of his early years with BSD.

As in the case with Samantha, Henry was a proactive part of the treatment process. He knows he wants to have the fewest days possible in an unstable state. Because he has been so active in learning about BSD and in understanding his symptoms, he can communicate very efficiently to help us help him regain mood stability. The total time of the follow-up calls (Henry to one of us, our conversations with each other, and then two follow-up calls) was probably under ten minutes. And because he was so resourceful about getting and adjusting his treatment, he missed very few days of work.

What About Your Treatment?

How do you make a decision that the medication you are taking now is working? Think about these questions:

- Do you feel less depressed? Less revved?
- Do you get more restless or feel calmer after a few days on or off the medication? Do you have fewer anxious thoughts?
- Are there changes in the tone of your voice, in the energy of your thoughts, or in the degree to which you can't get off a topic?
- Do you sleep more soundly, or are you having trouble falling asleep or staying asleep?

■ Do you feel more irritable or better able to take things in stride?

■ Can you think in a more flexible way, or do you feel as if every thought is emotional?

In Exercise 6 you can track your changing symptoms to help you sort out the benefits and costs of each change in medication. You will notice that the "patient" who filled out the sample sheet reports that he feels a little depressed and tired and has trouble concentrating. He is sometimes sleeping and eating too much. Are the problems with sleeping and eating really side effects from the medications? Or are they symptoms of continued depression?

He says he is feeling a little motivation. Is this an improvement or a decline? You can't know unless you track your symptoms—and see if you experience these symptoms before and/or after the medication.

Different Viewpoints on Your Health

Using this tracking sheet can help you communicate with your doctor and integrate different perspectives on the way you are progressing. To evaluate a particular trial of medication, doctors compare the state the patient is in once he or she has started on the new medication with the way they were before the medication. On the other hand, people with BSD tend to look to see the elimination of symptoms—they compare their current state with the state they were in before they got sick. These are different types of comparisons involving different time frames. So you may look better to your doctor but not feel better enough to yourself. Both points of view are important to consider. After all, in most cases, your doctor didn't meet you until after you got sick. So your doctor doesn't necessarily realize what has changed.

In addition, your doctor may be focused on one particular symptom—say, depression. You may be aware of remaining symptoms that still have not remitted or, in fact, have gotten worse because of the treatment. The tracking sheet can help keep the whole story in focus.

Your doctor is paying attention to a whole different set of symptoms—sort of the observable characteristics of BSD. This can include changes in your posture, your tone of voice, the pacing of your speech, your ability to make eye contact, the ways you express yourself, your irritability, and your sadness. It can be helpful to ask your doctor to pinpoint how he or she knows the medication is working (or is not).

You may be paying attention to the way you feel and to the personal goals you have (or have not) achieved. This point of view matters, too. And your treatment will benefit when your doctor understands your point of view.

Learning from Medication-Related Problems

Effective communication is the key. You and your doctor choose a course of action for the moment, and together you can articulate changes in symptoms that will let you know if you have made the right choice. For example, if you look depressed but are really in a mixed state, then antidepressants may make you more jumpy or cause you to have trouble sleeping. Your thoughts may feel more brittle or edgy.

Although it may be very uncomfortable, an increase in symptoms is a valuable piece of information. These symptoms provide you and your doctor with guidance about the nature of your diagnosis. With this information you and your doctor can make a course correction and develop more effective medication regimens over the long run.

Practical Considerations

It takes a lot of time and effort and close monitoring to learn to recognize the symptoms and develop strategies to control them. A single short (fifteen- to thirty-minute) visit every three months does not constitute effective monitoring. When our team (psychologists and psychiatrists) starts a new medication, we often talk to the patient within a few days (sometimes even the next day, depending on the medication). We make sure they are seen within a week. We teach them what to look out for, and we remain available as they increase the dose. It's worth doing this right. If you can't get to the doctor, then call. Or have a family member or therapist call for you, if you don't feel up to it.

A difficulty with this approach is that medication monitoring is not well reimbursed by insurance companies. You will have to work with your doctor to figure out the most cost-effective and safe way to stay closely monitored. The more you know about your symptoms and the side effects, the more efficiently (and cost effectively) you can communicate with the doctor.

The Most Important Message

Don't let the side effects slide. It doesn't make sense to call your doctor only when things have become dangerous or miserable. These medications can make tremendous improvements in your ability to function, but they require monitoring. If you see problems, don't hesitate to call your doctor.

Don't let the symptoms slide either. If you are not getting better or don't feel well, call. You are entitled to help.

One final note: many of our patients have very severe and uncomfortable symptoms, such as disabling anxiety, uncontrollable moods, and persistent suicidal thoughts. They cannot function without symptom control. Although there are many medication choices, sometimes the only medication that works for a particular person is one that causes significant weight gain or dampens sex drive. Sometimes it is necessary to accept some significant side effects in order to preserve life. No one likes it. But sometimes you face tough situations.

This is the way it is now. The pressure to develop better medications is very high, so we are confident that there are medications that will do better in the future.

EXERCISE 6
Medication Tracking Sheet

Write in 0 for not at all, 1 for a little, and 2 for a lot. (Note: you may feel more comfortable writing in your own words for the symptoms, as you practiced in Chapter 3.)

Here's an example:

	Date	Date	Date	Date	Date
	3/2/07				
Medications	Zoloft 50mg in the morning. Seroquel 200 mg at night.				
Symptoms					
Depressed mood	1				
Loss of interest or pleasure in activities	1				
Sleep					
Insomnia (difficulty sleeping)	0				
Hypersomnia (too much sleeping)	1				
Appetite					
Loss of appetite	0				
Increase in appetite	1				

Energy and movement					
Very low energy, fatigued	1				
Very slow movements	1				
Restlessness	0				
Worthlessness, guilt	1				
Poor concentration or indecisiveness	2				
Thoughts about harming or killing yourself	0				
Plans to kill yourself	0				
Inflated self-esteem or grandiosity	0				
Decreased need for sleep	0				
More talkative or pressure to keep talking	0				
Racing thoughts, flight of ideas	0				
Distractibility	1				
Increased activity					
Too much energy	0				
Lots of activity	0				
Too much involvement in pleasurable but potentially harmful activities (overspending, drug use, and gambling)	0				
Desire to be around other people to talk all the time	0				

Mood lability (mood changes very frequently or is very sensitive)	|				
Interpersonal hypersensitivity					
Can't stand being around people	|				
Very critical of yourself when you are with other people	|				
Keep worrying or thinking about your interactions with other people					
Feeling very anxious or very self-conscious around other people	|				
Additional symptoms you notice or improvement you experience					
More hopeful	0				
More comfortable	|				
Motivation to get things done	|				

Now it's your turn:

	Date	Date	Date	Date	Date
Medications					
Symptoms					
Depressed mood					
Loss of interest or pleasure in activities					
Sleep					
Insomnia (difficulty sleeping)					
Hypersomnia (too much sleeping)					
Appetite					
Loss of appetite					
Increase in appetite					
Energy and movement					
Very low energy, fatigued					
Very slow movements					
Restlessness					
Worthlessness, guilt					
Poor concentration or indecisiveness					
Thoughts about harming or killing yourself					
Plans to kill yourself					

Inflated self-esteem or grandiosity					
Decreased need for sleep					
More talkative or pressure to keep talking					
Racing thoughts, flight of ideas					
Distractibility					
Increased activity					
Too much energy					
Lots of activity					
Too much involvement in pleasurable but potentially harmful activities (overspending, drug use, gambling, etc.)					
Desire to be around other people to talk all the time					
Mood lability (mood changes very frequently or is very sensitive)					
Interpersonal hypersensitivity					
Can't stand being around people					
Very critical of yourself when you are with other people					
Keep worrying or thinking about your interactions with other people					
Feeling very anxious or very self-conscious around other people					

Additional symptoms you notice or improvement you experience					
More hopeful					
More comfortable					
Motivation to get things done					

Notes for the Family

Medication management is the key to recovery. But it is also the part of the treatment that feels most fraught with anxiety for the patient and the family. Family members often know that the patient must have some medical treatment, and yet they do not wish their loved one to experience side effects. They may be afraid the patient will get fat or dulled or zombielike. Family members can find themselves in the awkward and difficult position of having to side with the doctor or the patient, of having to voice their opinions about whether they believe medication and/or therapy is necessary for the patient. It can help to know that others are up against the same challenges. It is hard to accept that difficult treatment choices have to be made. But it is crucial to get everyone on the same side—believing in and working toward recovery.

Every psychiatrist and psychologist we have worked with has been torn about the costs and benefits of prescribing medications. On the one hand, the symptoms of BSD are dangerous and potentially deadly. We know that despite the patient's heartfelt wish that the symptoms would all go away with insight (or maybe a little Valium), symptoms are only likely to get worse unless they are treated with the proper medication.

And yet it is difficult to prescribe medications that are likely to cause weight gain, tremors, or slow thinking or that may deprive people of sexual pleasure. It is painful to have to explain to someone that he or she has a serious illness and may have to take serious medicines.

And for the physicians, this has to be done in an extremely tight time frame—usually fifteen- to thirty-minute visits, spaced over long time periods. But if people do not fully understand the nature of their disorder and its impact on their life, as well as the trade-offs involved in taking the medications, then it is hard to get good adherence to the medication regimens.

In most centers that treat cancer or diabetes or other serious illnesses, it would now be unacceptable to simply prescribe medications, hand out a pamphlet, and send the patient on his or her way. A program of symptom monitoring and psychoeducation and support is almost always offered. These programs help people and their families accept that something difficult has happened. Someone has gotten sick. The sickness causes certain symptoms and has certain treatments. People know that if they get cancer, they may have to take drugs that will make them nauseous, that will cause their hair to fall out, and so on. They work with their treatment team to understand and manage the trade-offs.

We try to create the same intensive treatment approach in our practice when working with a person who has BSD. We, the psychologists, work closely with the patient and psychopharmacologist to provide effective care. The communication between psychologist and psychiatrist helps ensure that we are addressing most symptoms and hearing about most of the side effects. We can each check our judgment about the course of treatment and make sure we are alert for signs of suicidality, for more serious side effects, and for oncoming stressors.

This communication is important, because things look different to each member of the team: the patient, the family, and each of the providers. From the psychiatrist's perspective, the situation is going well if the symptoms are reduced. From the patient's perspective, the situation is going well if his or her functioning has returned. From the family's perspective, the patient's happiness and safety are the most important goals—they have to take everything into consideration.

However, in many parts of the country, this kind of dual service (psychiatrist/psychologist) may be impossible to create. If this kind of intensive case management is not available, you can use educational materials to help you along. In fact, the reason that we wrote this book was because we were responding to the questions of families we met at National Alliance on Mental Illness (NAMI) meetings. Many people with BSD or who have family members with BSD just do not have access to the kind of care that is needed to manage a complex illness. A book or other educational materials can't really help you with the feelings you may have, but they can make you a more efficient and effective communicator. You can learn to think about the symptoms and learn the vocabulary you need to communicate with the doctor. And this knowledge can also make it a little easier to talk to other families and patients, to see similarities and get more support. You may be able to use chat rooms and local NAMI meetings to help you gain the kind of support and confidence that is necessary to keep moving forward. We know this kind of intensive support works for other kinds of chronic illness. Now we need to establish these standards of care for BSD as well.

Part 2

Problems and Solutions

I Just Don't Feel Like It

The Effects of BSD on Motivation

KEY POINTS

People with BSD often have difficulty starting and completing tasks.

They need much greater motivation to perform certain tasks, because the barriers to completion are higher.

The barriers are created by a combination of mood-regulation and information-processing problems.

Your ability to take effective action—to do things as simple as taking care of the laundry or planning a vacation—is affected by your mental status (your mood, level of anxiety, and ability to process information). When your mood is very low or you are very distracted by anxious thoughts, you will have trouble acting effectively.

When this happens, you just don't feel like doing anything. This is one of the most frustrating things about bipolar disorder. People are surprised and upset by how hard it is to get themselves to do the things that need to be done. DeShawn can't make himself clean the house. Solange can't get herself to open the mail and pay the bills until it is a real emergency. Lin can't seem to get to work on time, no matter how hard she tries.

Their symptoms are not uncommon. Some studies indicate that more than half of patients with BSD are unable to work or are able to work only in a sheltered setting. Persistent symptoms of depression, anxiety, or psychosis or a history of alcohol abuse make the risk for disability worse. However, clinically, it is our experience that with effective treatment, a systematic approach to symptom control, and a graded approach to work, it is possible to recover and to do what you set out to do.

Lack of Motivation

Like many other people with BSD, you may wonder what happened to your motivation. If you have been hypomanic or manic, you may remember a time when you were endlessly and effortlessly energized and motivated to succeed. Now, as you have trouble getting things done, you may be wondering if you are just not motivated. You may think, "If only I were really interested, I'd be motivated and then I could do something." Or, "If only I weren't so worried about my problems, then I could get my mind on my work and feel motivated to do something."

Depression and Motivation

Why do you seem to have so much trouble with motivation? Some of the difficulty getting started is a function of the particular symptoms of depression in BSD. For some people, depression may be accompanied by a leaden paralysis. Leaden paralysis is a way that psychiatrists describe the depression many BSD patients have: they can't move, they don't feel like they can do anything, they are stuck. This is one of the most difficult symptoms for patients and their families to understand. It can seem as if people are refusing to try or refusing to take action, that they simply aren't willing to help themselves. But really, they may be depressed—even if they don't feel very sad.

These symptoms of depression are a particular problem for people with BSD. Studies have shown that the more symptoms of depression people with BSD have, the less able they are to do what they are trying to do—for example, function as a wife or mother, husband or father, student or worker or friend. Almost all of our patients talk about times they just couldn't return a call, do the laundry, or get up to go eat breakfast. They just can't. And much of this difficulty doing things is a function of the depression part of their BSD.

Anxiety and Motivation

Sometimes anxiety can impair us as well. We all have had the experience of being so worried that we were too distracted to think straight or get anything done; our worries seem to get in the way of us doing anything. Maybe it was a time we were waiting for test results or worrying over someone we love. The problems arise when this bad mood or state of anxiety lasts a long time. In fact, people meet diagnostic criteria for a mental disorder when their internal state (mood or anxiety level) affects their motivation and behavior to the extent that they are no longer able to function effectively. In BSD the effects of anxiety can be debilitating. And as we will discuss in Chapter 9, information-processing problems can also make it more difficult for you to just get started.

The Desire to Try

But despite all these obstacles, most people with BSD keep trying. They keep pushing themselves to keep functioning—to take care of themselves, their families, and their work. They believe they will be able to achieve their goals if they have enough motivation to overcome the obstacles.

They know they need more motivation if there are more barriers to success. So when they have trouble getting themselves to do something, they may try to increase their motivation. They may try to make it more important to succeed or more scary to fail. They may tell themselves that their motivation reflects their values and character. Or they may try to find something that ignites a passionate interest, so they can use the emotion to motivate themselves to push past any difficulties. All in all, they try to get themselves to try harder—to get supermotivated to succeed. It just seems strange when you have to be supermotivated to take on even small tasks.

But the amount of motivation you need isn't the same as it was—the equation has changed. With BSD you are facing more obstacles to achieving your goals, even if you do not immediately recognize those obstacles.

Why do you need so much motivation? With BSD, the obstacles or barriers have increased. The underlying problems in mood regulation and information processing make even small tasks more difficult. These barriers can change the equation. They change the amount of motivation and the kinds of resources you need to start and complete tasks.

It can be painful to recognize that something that once was easy can now be hard to do, to recognize that your motivation is sometimes just not enough to overcome the obstacles. And this realization can make the situation worse if you become burdened with feelings of shame. But once you know how BSD affects motivation, you can systematically identify the resources you need to overcome these barriers.

Angela's Story

An example may help to clarify. Recently, Angela told me a story that helped me understand the way this struggle with motivation feels. Angela said that she had gone upstairs to remind her daughter, Gina, to do her math homework. She came back an hour later, only to find her daughter lying on her bed daydreaming. Angela asked Gina why she hadn't done her work, and Gina said, "I didn't feel like it."

At that moment, Angela realized that she had felt that way for a long time. *She just didn't feel like doing her whole life.* She didn't feel like getting up or doing her paperwork or cleaning the house or talking to other people.

And yet, what did she mean? Was it the same as what Gina meant? What Gina was really saying (although not out loud of course) is, "Mom, get out of here. I want to do other fun things more than I want to do math. In a little while, I'll get nervous about not finishing my homework in time, and I'll get to work."

Gina is procrastinating because what she wants to do is more interesting to her than what she has to do. If we ask her to rate her feelings about how hard it will be for her to do the math, she might say, "Well, on a scale of 1 to 10, I think the math is a little boring and a little hard, so it's about a 4."

As a mom, Angela thinks it is a sign of good character to be able to get your work done before you play. Because she feels like it is important to know how to get past your own human laziness, Angela pushes Gina to get started. She feels confident in her decision, because she knows that Gina can do her homework without a tremendous amount of difficulty. Put another way, Angela knows Gina can get going on the math if she pushes herself a moderate amount (about a 4 or 5).

Angela intuitively understands the relationship between mood, anxiety, and motivation, so she wonders if it works the same way for her. When she can't get her work done, when she doesn't feel like it—maybe she is just being lazy. Maybe if she just kicked herself, she could get started. Maybe she just has bad habits or bad character. Maybe if she had a passion for something, she could make herself function more effectively.

But it sure doesn't feel that way. Why not? Because her moods are more intense, she has more things to worry about, her thinking is not as clear or creative, and she is more tired. The amount of effort required to complete each task is much greater. Things that used to be a 4 are now a 9. Put another way, her underlying problems with mood regulation and information processing change the equation, so things are just harder to do. In Table 6.1 you can see the way these barriers affect the amount of motivation and effort you need to get things done.

Understanding Angela's Lack of Motivation. Let's examine each of Angela's chores to understand the relationship between motivation, symptoms, and behavior. We asked Angela to list the different things she had to do each day and to rate these activities on a scale from 1 (not at all hard to do) to 10 (very, very hard to do). Then we asked her to tell us if she got those tasks accomplished and if not, why not.

Here is what she said: "I can wake up and get my daughter off to school, even though it is very hard for me, because I am supermotivated to make sure she gets to school. Taking care of Gina is really the most important thing in my life. No matter how exhausted I am (and these medicines really make me tired), I make sure I get up and get her off to school."

She makes Gina's lunch and dinner for the same reason. She may make a very simple meal when she feels really bad, but she wants to

Table 6.1 How BSD Changes the Motivation Equation

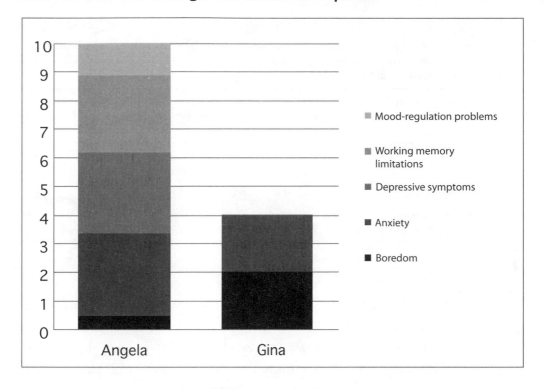

make sure food is on the table for her family. This is central to her identity and the meaning of her life.

Angela told me she is able to go to the grocery store now, because she has gotten used to it. She goes frequently so she doesn't have to do a lot of planning in advance; planning a once-a-week shopping excursion would be too overwhelming for her. She can just pick up what she needs for a day or two. She has problems with working memory and planning, but by breaking the shopping task into little pieces, she can get around those difficulties.

On the other hand, paying the bills and taking care of the insurance forms seems really overwhelming to her. Most people hate doing this kind of paperwork, and lots of people get frustrated and

Angela's Activity Ratings

Activity	How Hard Is It to Do? (scale from 1 to 10)	Did It Get Done?
Get up and get her daughter to school	6	Yes
Go to the grocery store	4 or 5	Yes
Pay the bills	9 or 10	No
Organize insurance forms	9 or 10	No
Call the insurance company	8 or 9	Called once but didn't get a resolution
Help her daughter with homework	5	Yes
Make dinner	4	Yes

upset submitting their insurance forms. But for Angela the job is especially difficult. She finds she just can't get herself to go into her study and take out the forms. She feels as if she must go to sleep as soon as she thinks she should get going on her paperwork.

Why are some things so difficult? Let's look at it from Angela's perspective. Just like anyone else, Angela thinks to herself, "Paperwork is boring. How many insurance forms can I fill out? Even if I finish this stack of papers, there are so many others that I have to do." But Angela is not just annoyed about being bored.

She knows that she is having some information-processing difficulties, specifically difficulties with her memory and thinking, common to many people with bipolar disorder (see Chapter 4). She worries about not having the concentration to complete a task. ("What if I start and can't finish? What if I get interrupted? Will I remember what I have done and be able to pick up where I left off?")

She is also worried that she will not be able to manage a telephone conversation with the insurance company if she has to resolve a dispute. She does not have confidence in her ability to remember what is being said to her and to be able to figure out on the spot what to do next. These are two tasks that are undermined by problems in working memory.

Negative Emotions. Angela has a whole range of negative emotions that further undermine her ability to concentrate. She is very worried about the outcome of filing the insurance paperwork. ("What if it doesn't work out? What if I don't get money back?") Her anxiety and mood-regulation problems make her emotional responses more intense and more prolonged than they would be for most other people. And she also feels sad and humiliated. Before she got so sick, handling these tasks would not have been a big deal for her. She wouldn't have given it much thought. Now these tasks seem overwhelming, and this makes her upset about the kind of person she is, the illness she has, her self-worth, and her future.

Because memories and thoughts are often stored along mood-related lines, thinking about one upsetting situation can trigger memories of other upsetting experiences. This roller coaster of negative ideas is more problematic for people with mood disorders. The chain of memories happens more quickly, and there are fewer positive memories easily available to serve as a kind of brake for the roller coaster of negative feelings. These feelings overwhelm the person's motivation.

Emotional and Physical Pain

It is important to remember that emotional pain is physical. When we feel negative emotions, we release cortisol and norepinephrine, among other neurohormones. These changes may physically manifest themselves as a racing heart, sweaty palms, or a dry mouth. But BSD may be accompanied by changes in the nervous system that make it difficult to recover or stabilize your emotional experience. In fact, laboratory studies show that individuals who tend to be anxious and depressed take a longer time to return to baseline—to recover physiological stability once they get activated.

It can be uncomfortable and distracting to have your body get so activated. For example, right after a good workout at the gym, your brain probably feels clearer. But it would be hard to settle down immediately to solve math problems or balance your checkbook. You might want some time for your body to quiet down, so you can concentrate on something outside yourself. In fact, that's why people like to listen to music while exercising. We need to distract ourselves from our internal state (our beating hearts, our panting breath, and so on). Therefore, to think clearly, it is important to be reasonably comfortable. And it is hard to be physically comfortable when you are very distressed. You just don't feel well.

Why You Really Don't Feel Like It

When you consider all these factors, you can see that the barriers to getting the job done have suddenly increased. And you can understand why Angela just doesn't feel like she can do the paperwork. If you look back at Table 6.1, you can see that Angela needs a lot more motivation to get over the hump of the barriers (or she needs some resources to help her manage the barriers more effectively).

When Angela says, "I don't feel like it," it has a new meaning. It means, "The feelings that could be there to motivate me—the pride in getting something done and the possibility of getting some money back—these positive feelings are not very strong. And they are drowned by the feelings of anger, anxiety, sadness, humiliation, and fear that come up when I try to do these simple tasks in my disabled state."

You and Your Motivation

Why can't you get motivated? You may be asking yourself, "Why don't I feel like doing it? Why can't I just go do it?" You might want to think about the different kinds of feelings you are having. You can try asking yourself, "What am I feeling when I am avoiding something?" It can be helpful to think about and break down the different kinds of feelings you are having.

Just knowing specifically how you feel can make it seem less unpredictable and less uncontrollable. It may be too hard to do this when you are actually having the feelings, but you can analyze the situation another time, when you feel a little better—or maybe when you are talking it over with someone.

It can also be helpful to remember that when you are doing something difficult (even if it is a small thing), you have the negative feelings at the time and the good feelings come later. So you have to be able to imagine and remember what it is like to feel satisfied and happy after completing a task. And that memory can be very weak if you are sick.

Try it yourself. Work on Exercise 7. You can use this analysis as a guide to help you decide what help you need. Think about what you have to do and how it feels for you to do it. Most of the time, people, unless they are supermotivated, will not do things that cost them more than a 4 on their own effort scale. You can use this understanding to help you when you get overwhelmed. Try to figure out what you really mean—and how high or low your motivation level is on the effort scale—when you say, "I don't feel like it."

In the next set of chapters, we will examine how problems with information processing and mood regulation can raise the barriers, and how you can work to get the resources you need to shrink them back down to size.

But first you have to recognize that sometimes you just don't feel like dealing with BSD. It's a tough problem, and it is hard to accept that you have gotten sick. BSD itself can make the problem harder by influencing the way you think about yourself.

EXERCISE 7
Your Activities: Charting the Effort Required

Write in the tasks you need to do on a daily basis and also some other harder things you have been avoiding. See if you can figure out why some tasks get accomplished and others don't.

Tasks You Need to Do	How Hard Does It Seem to Do the Task? (on a scale of 1 to 10)	Does the Task Get Done? (no, a little, mostly, yes)	If Not, What Makes It So Hard? (Does it require a lot of concentration? Does it make you anxious? Does it remind you of being sick? Do you need to talk with other people? Is it too big a job to do all at once?)

I Just Want Things to Go Back to the Way They Were

The Effects of BSD on Your Motivation to Recover

KEY POINTS

It can be hard to accept that you have a difficult medical disorder.

Everyday reminders of the difficulties you face can undermine your courage.

Depression can make your ideas about BSD inaccurate and catastrophic. These faulty beliefs can reinforce the depression.

Challenging these beliefs can help you succeed.

It can be very hard to accept having BSD. People who have BSD (just as is true for anyone who faces any significant medical diagnosis) have to face a change in the way they think about themselves and their future. They have to find a path toward recovery, setting new goals and appreciating different kinds of accomplishments.

It can be hard to accept the difficulties that come with any serious illness. You might feel overwhelmed as you think about the problems you face as a consequence of BSD. But the symptoms of

BSD can make it worse. Depression can color your thinking and make negative or catastrophic thoughts seem true.

In this chapter, we will use some of the techniques from cognitive-behavior therapy to help us evaluate our expectations and challenge inaccurate or catastrophic beliefs about BSD. You can use these strategies to help you gain the strength you need to cope with BSD.

Let's start by examining different kinds of thoughts and feelings people have about BSD. Two tables, appearing a little later in this chapter, list the specific thoughts people might have. In the left side of the tables are some of the extreme or worst-case versions of these thoughts, while the right side of the tables presents more reasonable alternatives.

"How Could This Happen to Me?"

The condition may make you so overwhelmed that you feel as if you will never recover. You may be so angry about the unfairness of it all that you want to refuse to participate in the work of recovery. And sometimes these feelings of anger, frustration, and sadness can get so strong that they can undermine your will to do the hard work necessary to recover. You may feel there is no point in trying, because things are so different from what you imagined. You may feel irreparably damaged when you compare the way you are now with the way you imagine "normal" people to be.

Worst of all, you can be so ashamed about getting sick that you start to feel unlovable. You may believe you somehow deserve this condition. You can start to view this illness as a product of spiritual or character failure and as a sign of weakness.

But it isn't. You didn't ask to get sick, and you don't deserve it. It happens, and you can recover. But it is easier if you see the situation for what it is, a situation in which you have a medical illness that affects many aspects of your life.

Let's look at the worst-case scenario thoughts in Table 7.1. Do you ever have these thoughts? You don't have to accept the worst-case scenario. If you put your catastrophic thoughts into words, you can see that they reflect feelings more than facts. These ideas are really examples of emotional reasoning, and they don't reflect an accurate picture of BSD.

See if you can think in a little less catastrophic way. Table 7.1 offers some examples. In Exercise 8, at the end of this chapter, you can write in your own worst-case scenario thoughts along with more reasonable alternatives. You can use this exercise to improve the situation by recognizing emotional reasoning and catastrophic thinking and then considering more reasonable alternative ideas.

Table 7.1 Catastrophic Beliefs About BSD and More Reasonable Alternatives

Worst-Case Scenario Thoughts	More Reasonable Ideas
"I don't believe I can recover, I just can't see it happening. I am so afraid of feeling devastated, I just can't think about it."	"I can recover. Other people have recovered. It is hard, but it is very possible."
"It is so unfair that I am sick. I am not going to do anything because it is so unfair."	"It is unfair. It is very frustrating. I am very angry and upset. I just don't want these feelings to stop me every time I try to make my life better."
"I am not normal. I can't stand the fact that I am not normal."	"It is true that I am sick, but I am still me, even if I can't always appreciate that. I am still important to the people who love me."
"I am so damaged, no one will want me."	"Actually, I know for a fact that people with BSD do develop meaningful relationships and they are still wanted and needed. It will get easier and more possible as I get better."

Triggers in Everyday Life

Everyday life can be filled with triggers or reminders of the difficulties you may face with BSD (that is, the ways your symptoms of BSD and the side effects of treatment affect your functioning and your quality of life). Sometimes these reminders will make it very hard to get started on the process of recovery, on the tasks you set for yourself.

Steve's Story

Let's look at an example. Steve wants to do the household cleaning chores. Because he is not working now, he wants to try to pull his weight in some way. He wants to get going, but he gets stuck—stuck pacing or reading novels or sleeping.

Steve was pretty mystified by his own behavior. He had always been a caring and responsible guy, but despite his best intentions, he just couldn't get himself started.

So we began to think about breaking the house cleaning into smaller pieces to make it easier for him to get started (for example, he could leave the vacuum out the night before or put the pail with the cleaning supplies right by the bathroom door). We broke the harder chores down into even smaller pieces (he could dust the shelves in the small bookcase and then dust the shelves one by one in the big bookcase). And this helped a little.

But it didn't quite get to the heart of the matter. So we talked some more and began to better understand the problem. When Steve wakes up and begins to think about his day, he realizes his primary responsibility right now is to clean the house. This is a depressing thought. Thinking about cleaning the house reminds him of how much he has lost since he got sick. When he was able to work, he had responsibilities that seemed much more meaningful to him. He had a cleaning lady who cleaned the house. This is clearly more than a lack of motivation (which we addressed in Chapter 6). His inability to clean the house was a symptom of a real blow he had suffered to his sense of self.

Ego Injuries

The losses of meaning and of pride are ego injuries, wounds to our sense of self. Steve knows that it is just housekeeping and not really the end of the world, but his unspoken thoughts have the power to make him feel very bad and stop him in his tracks. Steve does not yet have the mood stability and sense of accomplishment necessary to fight off the sadness or numbness he feels when these daily or routine ego injuries occur.

Table 7.2 lists some of the thoughts Steve had about his situation. He didn't realize these thoughts were even in his head until

Table 7.2 Steve's Thoughts

Worst-Case Scenario Thoughts	More Reasonable Ideas
"I used to have a cleaning lady, and now I can't afford one. I am a failure."	"I am not working now, but I think I will be able to work in the future. Even if I can't work now, it doesn't take away all the things I have accomplished in my life."
"I can really notice the tremors that I have when I do the cleaning. These medications and this illness make me an old man."	"I have to take the medications, but if I am having tremors, I can talk to my doctor. Maybe she can fix this problem."
"I can't take care of my wife—I am not really a man anymore."	"At our wedding, we said that we would take care of each other through sickness and health. I need some attention now. I hope it never happens, but I will take care of her if she ever needs it."
"I am a bad and selfish person because I can't make myself do these things."	"No, I am just having some trouble with depression. I couldn't be bad and selfish, because I am working so hard to get this problem fixed."

he started to talk about them. And then he was able to think them through in a less frightening and more practical way. (By the way, now that he knows he gets overwhelmed by these thoughts, he turns up some Irish music and gets going on the chores.)

Every day most people suffer some of these losses: you get criticized by your boss, your wife yells at you, you burn the dinner. Most of the time, you get over it and bounce back. But when you have a mood disorder, these ego losses can be much harder to take. The losses can pierce your heart.

Sometimes it may not even be clear that it is an ego injury you are experiencing. You may not be fully aware that you feel sad or angry or afraid. If you haven't thought things through, you may be catastrophizing—feeling worse or thinking things are worse than they are. But you can't even reevaluate your thinking if you don't realize you are thinking these things.

BSDs and the medicines prescribed for BSDs can cause some physical and psychological changes that may make you feel less powerful, less competent, less sexy, and less physically strong. The changes that actually occur may be much less significant than your emotional responses to these changes. And you may get overwhelmed by the emotional responses to these changes without even realizing that this has happened and without having the opportunity to challenge your own ideas. A little preparation can help.

When you find yourself feeling unable to do something, you can ask yourself if the situation is in some way reminding you of the loss of any of the following:

- your masculinity (or femininity)
- power (being the provider or the "chief" at home or work)
- physical strength or coordination

It is often extremely helpful to make a list of some of the thoughts you might have. Exercise 8, at the end of the chapter, provides you with some space to write down your own thoughts and to write down more reasonable alternatives.

Depression and the Desire to Recover

Depression can make you feel as if the negative thoughts about living with BSD are true, and the thoughts can reinforce your depression. It can be critical to talk these issues over with your doctors to make sure you are challenging any inaccurate beliefs.

But it isn't as simple as changing the sentences. Talking through these thoughts can help you realize what you are saying to yourself (maybe not consciously, but somewhere in the back of your mind). But much of what is happening is still painful.

It takes a stable mood to be able to tolerate the daily triggers of distress and to develop new sets of life goals. When your mood is not well regulated, it can be too painful to accept these difficulties and very hard to develop more reasonable plans. As your mood stabilizes, it will be easier for you to figure out how you want to handle the BSD.

Most important, it takes a high level of support to tolerate the change in your life. It can be helpful to share your worries with your doctor. Your doctor won't be surprised. Most people with BSD have these thoughts and feelings. We have a group for BSD, and the group members support each other in setting and tolerating new goals. It can take the edge off some of the pain to know that other people (other likable, intelligent, and motivated people) are in the same position.

EXERCISE 8
Reconsidering Your Thoughts About BSD

Write in your own worst-case scenario thoughts. Try to include some daily triggers (thoughts you might have while going about your daily routine). These are thoughts that come up when you see the way BSD affects you in your daily life. Then write in some more reasonable alternatives. If you can't think of a more reasonable approach or are having trouble putting your worst fears into words, do this exercise with someone you care about and trust.

Your Worst-Case Scenario Thoughts	More Reasonable Approaches

I Don't Know Where to Begin

Setting Goals with BSD

KEY POINTS

Making progress requires setting realistic goals.

Setting realistic goals requires that you evaluate your condition accurately.

Symptoms of BSD can affect your ability to see yourself and your situation clearly.

Getting feedback from others you trust can help you set achievable goals.

It takes real success and real achievement to feel better. But one of the most difficult challenges is setting reasonable goals. The mood-regulation and information-processing problems associated with BSD can make it necessary for you to work toward your personal and professional goals at a slower pace. If you are a student, you may need to take fewer courses as you recover. If you are working, you may have to reduce your workload or adjust your responsibilities so you have less stress. As is the case with most chronic illnesses, recovery from BSD depends on slow and steady accomplishment, combined with careful stress management. You want to build on real success.

Accepting this slower pace can feel demeaning and dispiriting. It can feel like accepting defeat at the hands of an unknown and mysterious enemy—an enemy that seems to be undermining your drive to succeed and your joy in life. A realistic evaluation of your condition can help you cut this enemy down to size.

Setting Realistic Goals

At times it's hard to know how to be realistic. It's hard to know what expectations make sense. You know things have changed. You have a sense of what you can't do, but you don't know what you will be able to do. You can't count on doing the things that made you feel proud before (or maybe you never got a chance to accomplish things you hoped would make you proud). And you don't yet know what accomplishments are ahead of you. You need information to help you develop new dreams and new expectations.

Achieving real success requires setting achievable goals. This can be the most difficult part. You have to develop a new way to think about your goals and accomplishments. And you have to challenge your catastrophic or inaccurate beliefs about setting new goals.

A number of beliefs can undermine your ability to set reasonable goals. You may believe that if you acknowledge your limitations, you are committing yourself to disability. You may believe that if you accept the limitations, you can't agree to fight them. You may be afraid that you will never push yourself.

But you don't have to deny the problems to succeed. You can look the problems straight on and find new ways to rise to the challenge of facing them.

Ruby's Story

Let's look at an example. Ruby used to be an executive. Once she got sick, she just couldn't get started building a new life. She only wanted to return to her high-powered, fast-paced job. When I recommended she start out with simpler, less-stressful tasks, like volunteering or working part-time, she felt angry and insulted. She thought I was treating her like she is "damaged goods."

Even though she knows she won't be able to tolerate working full time in a high-level position, she feels she must say that she can do it. Saying that she can't is akin, in her mind, to completely giving up to BSD. And yet, if she doesn't accept some limitations and start somewhere, she won't get started at all. She is having trouble tolerating the comparison between her current condition and the way she remembers herself when she wasn't so sick.

Like Ruby, you can be so distressed and frightened about having BSD that you aren't able to realistically evaluate your situation. Look at Table 8.1 to see some of the underlying thoughts that Ruby might have had and see if we can challenge them with more reasonable alternatives.

Why is Ruby giving herself such a hard time? She is experiencing the pain associated with social comparison; she is comparing who she is now to her idea of a more perfect person or perfect situation.

When you ask yourself "Am I as good as other people?" or "Am I as good as I was before I got sick?" you are engaged in social comparison.

Social Comparisons

When you ask these questions, you are engaged in social comparison. Sometimes social comparisons can be motivating, such as when you find yourself doing something that someone else in your position can't do or something that you yourself couldn't do the week before. However, sometimes when you see the difference between what you do and what you can imagine you do, you experience what we call an ego injury. As we have discussed, an ego injury is an

Table 8.1 Reasonable Thoughts About Setting Goals When You Have BSD

Worst-Case Scenario Thoughts	More Reasonable Ideas
"If I accept that I am sick, I will never get better."	"If I accept that I am sick, I can get the treatments I need to get better."
"If I take a part-time job, I will never work full time again."	"I might have to take a part-time job now. But if it goes OK, I can move toward full time in the future."
"If I accept a lower position, I'll never do anything at work. I am so exhausted that if I am not supermotivated by the money or prestige, I will never do anything."	"I may be exhausted, but if I take one step at a time and pace myself, I can accomplish something."
"If I try a simpler task and can't perform it, I won't be able to handle the humiliation."	"I have to take a risk sometime. I will ask for help if I need it."
"If I set lower goals, I won't seem attractive to other people."	"I will still be important to the people I love, even if I stop being so ambitious. It is probably better to actually get something done than to just talk about it."
"If I go slow, I will be a loser."	"If I succeed, even if it takes me longer and even if I don't accomplish everything I set out to do (and who does?), I will be a winner."

injury to the way you think about yourself, to the idea of yourself that you keep in your mind and your heart.

The Best Self You Can Be

We all have an internalized image of ourselves as the best self we can be. And we use those internal images (some psychological theories call them internal objects, because they are so real) to guide our own behavior. We want to be a certain way, and the awareness of the gap between what we are doing and that ideal self makes us uncomfortable, so we have the motivation to take action. For example, I want to be a good mother, and I have a vision of what me as a good mother would look like (calm and patient), and so that vision (some-times) stops me from screaming at the kids when they do something wrong. My daughter wants to be a really good musician, and that picture of herself as a really good singer makes her stay in the prac-tice rooms, even when she would really like to chat on the phone with her friends. And when she sloughs off on her practicing, she feels guilty because she knows that she is not living up to being the person she wants to be.

So when we see the gap between what we have done and what we wish we did—for example, when I find myself yelling at my daughter, or when she finds herself wasting away an afternoon on the telephone instead of practicing her scales—we feel uncomfort-able, maybe a little nervous, guilty, ashamed, or embarrassed. And these are feelings most people want to avoid. For most people, trying to avoid these ego injuries helps keep them on track. For people with BSD, these injuries can push you off track.

Depression and Social Comparison

Depression, including bipolar depression, makes you more likely to engage in negative social comparisons—to compare yourself to oth-ers, to the way you were before BSD, or to an idealized version of yourself. And in turn these comparisons make you more likely to feel upset and depressed. Sometimes the ego injuries can be devas-tating, too devastating for you to keep moving. Some individuals with BSD will avoid taking any risks or engaging in any activities that present a threat of an ego injury.

Social comparison can lead to damaging ego injuries when you have an unrealistic vision of what you are able to do. Your capacity may be temporarily changed by BSD. It is important to adjust your expectations according to the reality. You will recover functioning and gain new abilities and skills. But be aware that you may some-times have unrealistic expectations about the pace of recovery.

Sometimes just acknowledging and understanding those feelings can help them shrink in size and become less overwhelming. Sharing these feelings with others can sometimes help as well. Research shows that for many people (but not all) social support reduces distress and reduces the physiological arousal that accompanies distress, making the intensity lower.

Sometimes people are more willing to take risks when they feel supported by other people, even if they are not right in the room. When we discuss these issues in our BSD support group, our patients say that simply seeing that other people face the same challenges is helpful. Sometimes the members call each other for support; this reduces the size of the barriers to setting achievable goals.

Not-So-Realistic Goals

But there's one more issue, particular to BSD, that makes setting goals a little more complicated.

It can be hard to accept that your goals and expectations may not have been realistic to begin with. You may need to understand the ways that BSD has shaped your ideas about yourself. The symptoms of BSD can create some of the difficulties in setting reasonable goals.

How? Your sense of self is connected to your feelings—your feelings about your goals, accomplishments, and failures. BSD pretty dramatically affects the way you feel about yourself. In turn, the way you feel about yourself influences your expectations for success and your evaluation of progress—the way you compare yourself to your ideal self or to other people.

How do these moods affect your ability to set reasonable goals? Like many people with BSD, you may have become very focused on the self-image you developed during a hypomanic or manic period.

You may have seen yourself as powerful, competent, and confident. And you may have been more productive than usual. Unfortunately, if you were manic, this could have been an illusion.

But you may still long for that positive self-image to be restored. The glossy images of yourself that may have developed during a hypomanic period are more like advertising copy than real life. These images are naturally more attractive than a depressed version of yourself and are more attractive than an everyday view of yourself. (In fact, many people with BSD say they never want to be ordinary or mediocre. Thinking of themselves as ordinary feels so different from the self-image they have when they are hypomanic.)

Kwame's Story

Let's look at an example. Kwame is in danger of losing his job as a graphic artist in an advertising agency. When he first came to therapy, he would say, "If I could just get my confidence back, I could do anything." But that "confidence" he missed so much was really just part of being manic.

Kwame believed his current problems were really a kind of depression or low self-esteem. He wanted to take antidepressants and learn to think better things about himself. But his confident self-image was not completely realistic.

When he was hypomanic, he felt like he could do anything, but he wasn't really able to do all the things he believed he could do. He kept overreaching and taking on jobs that were beyond his training. He had not really acquired the technical and management skills he needed before he got sick. When he did not have the skills he needed to do the job, he would get overwhelmed and sleep and end up missing important meetings or failing to complete important assignments. This is why he got put on probation at work. Now he has some information-processing difficulties and mood-stability problems that make it more difficult for him to learn the skills he needs. He is certainly bright enough to learn these skills, although he will have to go slower.

Kwame is right that depression is making him feel less competent. But he is not just missing a feeling of realistic achievement. He is also missing the distorted feelings of competence and confidence he had when he was hypomanic. He is struggling with the need to accept that he will have to go slower—to accept this difference between the way he thought of himself and a more realistic self-appraisal.

Kate's Story

Let's look at one more example. Kate headed off to business school filled with great expectations and high ambitions. She wanted to graduate with straight As, go to work at an investment bank, earn tons of money for a few years, and then retire to become a full-time mom.

During the first semester, she had a very hard time and experienced a relapse of her symptoms. I asked her if she would be allowed to take a reduced course load and if she would consider trying that approach. She said she had permission to take a reduced load but that she would never do it.

Why not? Kate said she knew some other people who were going to school part time. But, she said, "They can go slow, they had reasons. The students going part time were young mothers, and they needed to go slower so they could take care of their kids." I pointed out that she had a reason, too. She has a BSD, and that can make it necessary to take things more slowly.

Kate rejected BSD as a reason to go to school part time. She told me she could not stand to have other people know she needed help or to see that she needed to go more slowly. She felt like she would be branded as a loser and would not be on the fast track. She wouldn't be able to keep to her plans for her future.

How did Kate get so stuck that she was unable to accept taking a reduced course load? Like everyone, Kate's ideas about herself and her capabilities blossomed out of her emotions and desires. But hypomanic feelings of confidence created a shiny, artificial, unrealistic self-image. Her elevated mood prevented her ambitions from being modified by experience, tempered by real-life successes and failures. Instead, her emotions created an image of success, and her feelings ensured that she inadvertently got more committed to this image.

The images she had of her successful future left out the actual details—what it feels like to work very hard at an intense pace for that long, especially while dealing with a difficult disorder. These images reminded us of the movies—you may see something bad, but you don't really feel it or smell it. In a way, the mood separated the ideas and images from real thinking.

Kate feels intense shame and humiliation about her failure to achieve these goals. She would rather drop out than try again at a reduced load. Her sense of pride prevents her from being willing to take steps along the way to achieving her long-term goals. She is not yet able to accept that she has certain limitations, some of which are related to her BSD. She swings back and forth between optimistically believing she could do it (if she could only get motivated) and feeling abject despair because she cannot work up the motivation. This is a miserable place to be. For Kate, pride is the enemy of progress.

But it's easy to understand Kate's perspective. She is smart and ambitious, and as soon as she started her career, she got sick. It is pretty devastating to get seriously ill. You probably have a tremendous desire to just "get back to normal." You may find it very painful to see people who don't have BSD or to see people who knew you before you got sick. You may feel too angry and frustrated to slow down enough to plan for recovery.

So to battle your pride, it may be worth thinking through both your goals and the sentences you say to yourself as you hit road-blocks. When you think through your goals in Exercise 9, you are using diagnostic skills to check out the quality of your thinking. You may have a feeling about success or an image of yourself as a successful person. These images may feel very right and true. You may not realize that you haven't fully fleshed out what you want to accomplish.

We will say it again. The best antidote to this problem is a close relationship. It can be very hard to accept that we may be less than we wished to be. Everyone has to face this at some point in life. But a close and loving relationship—with a therapist, a family member, a friend, a coworker, a doctor, or a clergyman or anyone else who is important to us can remind us that we count. We all need someone who can remind us that it is worth it, that we still matter, even if we don't achieve all our ambitions. A close relationship can help you to be able to accept limitations without losing hope. Love and care can provide the motivation to keep working day-to-day and step-by-step to achieve your goals.

Choosing Goals

Understanding how your self-reflection can vary with your mood can help you understand the fundamental nature of bipolar disorder. You may not be able to change the way you think about your goals right away, but you can track it. You should see changes both in the detailed nature of your goals and in the underlying thoughts you have about achieving these goals.

Following are some questions you can answer to help you evaluate your goals. Think about your ambitions.

- Do you dream very grand and very small (for example, running the company and staying at home)?
- Do you dream of taking on major responsibilities at the same time you are dreaming about letting it all go, having a life with very limited responsibilities?
- Are you afraid of being exhausted but also afraid of being a failure?

If you have very glossy goals and can't think through the details, hypomania may be influencing your judgment. If you are simultaneously ambitious and very worried about being exhausted, then it is worth considering the possibility that you have some underlying depression. Share these thoughts with your doctor.

EXERCISE 9
Identifying Goal-Setting Thoughts

See if you can identify the thoughts you are having as you try to set goals for yourself. Think about your ultimate goals. Then think about possible intermediate steps. If you can't reach your ideal goal now, what would be an intermediate goal, an alternative short-term goal? What are your thoughts and feelings about reaching for a midpoint, a less ambitious or glamorous goal? Or taking a longer time to reach your goals?

Here's an example:

Your Long-Term Goal	Your Dream Short-Term Goal	An Alternative Short-Term Goal	Your Worst-Case Scenario Thoughts About Setting This Alternative Short-Term Goal	A More Reasonable Way of Thinking
Be a successful investment banker.	Go to business school full time and graduate with honors.	Take fewer courses each term.	"I'll be a loser; no one will ever employ me."	"Actually, there are plenty of people who go to school part time and plenty of people who don't work at the top firms—and they still earn a living."
		Work for a year until mood stabilizes and then start school part time.	"I'll be too old; no one will take me seriously. I can't be a star if I am old."	"Actually, a lot of people return to work after a period of time away, and I really will only be a year older."

Now it's your turn:

Your Long-Term Goal	Your Dream Short-Term Goal	An Alternative Short-Term Goal	Your Worst-Case Scenario Thoughts About Setting This Alternative Short-Term Goal	A More Reasonable Way of Thinking

Here's an important point. If you have a lot of trouble breaking down the goals into steps and just want to get to the finish line, you may be having racing thoughts. This "speediness" may make it hard to think things through carefully. Or you may just end up feeling overwhelmed or very anxious or angry. Your mood may not be stable enough to tolerate the ego injuries that are part of completing this task. And that may be why you can see a goal but can't get started down the path toward achievement. If you have these symptoms, it's a good idea to talk to your doctor.

In the next two chapters, you will learn in a little more detail about how mood-regulation and information-processing problems contribute to your difficulties setting and achieving your goals.

Notes for the Family

One of the most difficult issues for many families is working through the pain and rage that people have about getting sick. Lots of times these feelings get expressed as anger at the family or other loved ones. If you advocate a slower pace, the person with BSD may feel that you have given up on him. If you don't accept his pace, he may feel you don't understand or accept him.

Understanding BSD takes time for everyone: the patient, the doctor, and the family. It can be really confusing to understand what is happening. When you are talking to your family member with BSD about goals or activities, it can be helpful to get in the habit of "speaking the subtext," as one patient said to me. It can be useful to say what's on your mind.

For example, the father of a young woman with BSD keeps yelling at her to shape up, to clean up her room, to get busy, and so on. He is yelling because he is so frightened. He doesn't really understand why she is having so much trouble moving forward. He can't tell if she has bad character or if she is sick. He is afraid that he will let her down if he doesn't push her. And at the same time, he is afraid of destroying her with his temper.

If you are nagging or yelling, it may be helpful to put your underlying thoughts and feeling into words. Speak the subtext. Ask about the goals and intentions of the person with BSD. Ask her why she is having trouble. Work together to try to figure out how to support each other—to figure out when you should push, when you should help her break down the task, and when you should just accept that some things might be too hard right now. Just listening to the experience may be the most important thing to do.

My Mood Affects Everything I Do

How Mood Regulation Affects Your Functioning

KEY POINTS

BSD involves problems with the quality, intensity, and stability of your mood.

BSD can affect the ability to shift your attention away from negative or high-intensity thoughts and feelings.

These mood problems can affect your information processing.

Mood problems can make it difficult to tolerate being around other people.

Mood problems can make it hard to self-reflect and regulate your own behavior.

The core symptoms of BSD involve problems with mood regulation. As we have been discussing, with BSD you are likely to have problems with the quality of your mood, even when you are not in a manic or depressed episode. You may not feel well, you may feel somewhat off kilter, and more specifically, you may often feel depressed. You may have problems with the intensity of your moods—you may feel too much elation or too much depression or anger. And you may have problems with the stability of your moods. Your feelings may seem erratic, too responsive to different situations, either real or anticipated. Once an intense feeling occurs, it tends to take over, making it difficult to shift attention away from the distressing (or too exciting) thoughts.

These mood problems can sometimes be the hardest symptoms to recognize. They can seem like features of your personality or a function of the circumstances of your life at the moment. You may think any of these things: "I am not having racing thoughts. I am just excited and creative and confident." "I am not irritable. This situation is just ridiculous—anyone would be annoyed by this person." "I am not stuck. There is just no acceptable way to solve this problem. I have to keep thinking about it to find a way to solve it."

After all, just like everyone else, people with BSD get sad or happy or angry or worried depending on what's happening. But there may be BSD symptoms at work that make a tough situation worse. Recognizing mood-regulation symptoms is the key to successful recovery.

Mood-Regulation Problems

Mood-regulation problems affect most aspects of your life, because thoughts and emotions are intertwined. Each of our thoughts is "attached" to some emotional experience. Think about almost anything, and you will realize that you have an emotional response to it. Think about lemons or a scary movie you enjoyed, and you feel things in your body (maybe your mouth starts to pucker when you think about lemons or your heart rate increases a bit when you think of the movie).

And it goes the other way as well. Our mood influences the content of our thoughts. If we are in pain, we are more likely to focus on negative thoughts. If we are in a manic state and elated, we are more likely to pay attention to thoughts about the benefits of our actions and less likely to pay attention to thoughts about the negative consequences.

In BSD, problems with mood regulation can affect thoughts about each aspect of our life—the way you think about yourself, your work, and your interactions with others. Moods can influence your insight, your ability to think about yourself in an accurate way or regulate your own behavior. They can affect your ability to get started and keep going on important tasks. And they can make it very difficult to tolerate being with other people. Let's examine each issue in turn and see what we can do about it.

Mood Regulation and Your Sense of Self

Our mood affects our thoughts about ourselves, not only what we think but also our willingness to self-reflect. When you are hypomanic or manic, you may feel supremely confident and highly competent. You may have these good feelings about yourself, even when they aren't necessarily accurate.

In a hypomanic or manic state, you may not be able to self-reflect accurately. You may not even be aware that your self-perception is colored by your emotions. The elated mood may turn your attention away from warning signs, and racing thoughts will distract you from serious self-reflection. In Chapter 7, we talked about the ways hypomania can also influence your concepts about yourself and your memories about your past accomplishments. You may be most likely to remember those ideas and events that are consistent with your elevated mood at the time you were hypomanic.

When you are depressed, the situation changes. As we have discussed, you may start to feel very bad about yourself and lose confidence. You are more likely to start comparing yourself to other people or to an ideal self. When you see a gap between the way you are and the way you think things should be, you experience an ego injury. When you are depressed, the pain from those ego injuries doesn't motivate you. Instead, it can derail you.

The underlying mood disorder makes it hard to recover well from these ego injuries. So it may not work to push yourself to try harder by being self-critical. ("Come on, don't be so lazy.") In fact, as you've seen in the last two chapters, these self-criticisms often don't just fail to motivate you, they can hurt you.

The irritability of a mixed state and the pain of depression can make it intolerable to self-reflect (that is, to think about yourself and your work). Accepting criticism can be very difficult for you, because it triggers unpleasant thoughts and feelings. It can unleash a river of self-hatred or self-doubt. To avoid this pain, you may become very defensive in your interactions with other people or even in the ways you review situations in your own mind. The difficulty is that it is almost impossible to learn and grow without being able to self-reflect and to correct your course when things are not going well.

Lauren's Story. Let's look at an example of the ways in which your mood can make certain kinds of self-evaluations too painful and ineffective. Lauren is a high-level executive who has bipolar II. When she gets depressed, the first set of symptoms she has is a series of negative thoughts about herself. She will come into the session repeating old ideas she has about her competence, her ability to negotiate the world, and her ability to tolerate the stresses and strains of a competitive corporate environment. The content of her thoughts is similar to the kinds of concerns many executives must have: "Am I getting the recognition I deserve?" "What does it take to get noticed by the boss?"

When her mood is reasonably stable, she can discuss these issues in a reasonable way—coming up with strategies for handling certain problems, recognizing her own strengths, and dispassionately evaluating the strengths and benefits of working for her company. But when Lauren is starting to move into a more depressed or mixed state, these thoughts take on a life of their own. She can't step back from the ideas and repeats her self-hating and self-defeating thoughts with absolute conviction. She hears the thoughts in her head as, "I never get the recognition I deserve. Other people who act badly get all the credit. There is nothing I can do to change my situation." She ruminates about these issues and is unable to take action or to feel anything but desperate and frustrated.

Now she recognizes that when she feels committed to these beliefs, it is time to call the doctor. She is starting the descent into an unstable mood state. And this recognition has helped her break the bipolar cycle. She doesn't spend so much time sinking into a depressed or mixed state. She works with her psychopharmacologist until she is able to stabilize her mood. Then she can develop more practical methods for facing the battles at work.

■ **Outside Opinions.** It can be very hard to realize you are not seeing yourself clearly. It takes a long time to understand how your mood regulates your sense of self. It can be important to work closely with your therapist or with friends and family to check in about the way you are thinking.

But we won't pretend this goes smoothly. The thoughts you have in these mood states have the ring or feeling of truth. You are unlikely to believe anyone else's version of who you are. So you may go through some trial and error until you find someone you can trust to give you accurate feedback about the way you are thinking about yourself.

Mood Regulation and Setting Goals

Mania, mixed state, and depression can all influence your ability to get started on important tasks or to continue working when you hit a snag of some sort. In addition, the effects of mood on your self-awareness can influence your productivity, because it is hard to start and finish your work without spending some time thinking about how you are doing. If you are hypomanic and your mood is too elated and you feel superconfident, you may feel bursts of creativity or excitement. Racing thoughts and flights of ideas are two of the symptoms of hypomania that can make you feel very creative (and actually be very creative). But these same racing thoughts can move too quickly to allow you to concentrate on working out the details.

Racing thoughts will make it hard to do the kind of task analysis that is needed to make plans to accomplish your goals. When your thoughts are moving too fast, it can be hard to slow down enough to finish meaningful sentences. You might find it difficult to think logically or practically about different issues. You may feel that you don't have the concentration to work out the details even when you know you have the start of a good idea. Your thoughts will move rapidly from idea to idea instead of concentrating on a sustained theme.

It's hard to notice when your thoughts are racing. You may feel as if ideas are moving rapidly through your mind. You can feel the hint of brilliance in your ideas, even if they are not fully formed. You may chain together ideas that feel right or feel like they make sense even when they might not. This may not be an unpleasant experience, but it still may interfere with your productivity and ability to function in a meaningful, practical way. To others you may seem as if you are talking quickly or dramatically or changing topics frequently.

Let's look at an example. Gene is writing a novel. He is full of feeling and ideas about the adventures his main character will take. But once he has a rush of ideas, he gets so excited that he cannot work in a sustained way. He feels like a kid in a candy store when he starts to imagine new characters and chapters. This excitement overwhelms his ability to stay focused and actually write down the ideas that have overtaken him.

Sonja's Story. You can have similar problems when you are in a mixed state, but the experience will feel more difficult. For example, Sonja is a college student with bipolar disorder who has been able to function very well with her medications. She is a very smart young woman who has just discovered how much she loves to study poetry. The excitement she feels about her classes, combined with the anxiety produced by the deadlines, is causing her to have a mild relapse. When she came home from school to see me, she was in a mixed state. Her symptoms included racing thoughts, combined with a very negative mood and a lot of anxiety.

She had a term paper to write, and as she talked about her paper, I could practically see the thoughts flashing across her mind. She talked all about the topic, making new connections between ideas even as she sat in my office. She felt capable of writing a brilliant paper, but she was frustrated and stymied because she could barely finish a sentence. She started the conversation with a great idea, but then her thoughts traveled elsewhere, and the great idea took off without her. Because she was so anxious, she felt like she was running at full speed on the inside but was paralyzed on the outside.

■ **Behavioral Activation System and BSD.** These symptoms may reflect problems in the behavioral activation system. Some researchers think this is a core deficit of bipolar. Both good events and bad trigger symptoms because the person cannot appropriately regulate the feelings they have in response to ideas or activities. So instead of getting just excited enough to feel motivated to sit down and work, you get so excited that you feel disoriented and exhausted—a little like a kid at a birthday party. The problem is that once you get too excited, you can't slow down your thinking enough to put one sentence after another.

If you are filled with great ideas but can't seem to get anything down on paper or can't work out any systematic plans, then you might consider the possibility that you are slightly hypomanic, even if it doesn't feel that way. It might be a good idea to bring these issues to your doctor's attention.

Mood Regulation and Being with Other People

If you have been hypomanic or manic, you may remember being very gregarious and charismatic. You may have been the center of attention, and you may have loved it. But often outside that time, most of our patients feel very uncomfortable being around people.

This discomfort can be a very limiting part of the disorder. It is hard to work effectively when you are uncomfortable with others. It can limit your family's ability to socialize when you can't interact. You can feel very lonely and isolated when you can't tolerate being with others. This is especially problematic because being around other people is precisely what people with BSD often need to help monitor and regulate their symptoms.

The difficulties being with other people can come from many sources. Bipolar II is associated with heightened interpersonal sensitivity. With bipolar II you may want to keep away from people to avoid the electric heat of embarrassment or the vibrating anxiety and edgy anger that you can feel when you have a conflict with someone else. Sometimes just thinking about conflict can make these feelings rush through your body. These thoughts can take on a quality of obsessionality, and it can be hard to focus your thoughts elsewhere.

Lucia's Story. Let's look at some examples of the ways that a mixed state can increase your interpersonal hypersensitivity. Lucia once came to my office after having a work dinner with colleagues and friends. She had been responsible for making the reservations at the restaurant, and when she and her guests arrived, the table they expected wasn't available. Lucia felt very disappointed and nervous about the way things were turning out. She had been so anxious and disappointed that she was preoccupied during the dinner. And then she was anxious after the dinner, worried that she had not handled the situation graciously.

Lucia had an ideal image—being a flawless and charming host in a glamorous restaurant with no hitches in the service or food. When she realized that she wasn't living up to this idea, her thoughts became obsessional. She thought again and again about what she could say that would make things right. The energy behind her worries was so distressing and distracting to her that Lucia couldn't stop thinking about how she would have to control every future event in intense detail so that something like this would never happen again. If she wasn't able to control these details, she thought to herself, then there was no point in attending any social event at all.

It's easy to see how dealing with other people can be affected by a change in your mood. As your mood stabilizes, however, this preoccupation with yourself and your image will fade. It will become much easier to accept "the slings and arrows of outrageous fortune" and of your contact with other people.

Mixed state can also make you much more irritable. Irritability in an interpersonal setting can be damaging to relationships. You may not even be aware of how much anger you are communicating. Other people are likely to notice and want to avoid encountering your razor tongue or angry tone. If you can tolerate it, you may want people to let you know when you are getting irritable. It can serve as a warning signal that helps you get the help you might need.

Depression and Interpersonal Relationships. Depression can also make it hard to be around others. You can feel completely internally preoccupied and overfocused on managing the BSD. You may not have any energy left for other people. You may wish to avoid shame or discomfort if you feel sick when others seem well. Information-processing problems can make conversations difficult, particularly if they are about sharing information.

So all in all, when you are in a depressed or mixed state, you may feel like you should avoid situations that will cause you to feel so self-aware or so instantly distressed. Many times this makes sense. When you are not well, reducing stress helps. But there may also be times when it is good to interact with others and to figure out how to gradually get back into the social swing. Thinking through some examples may help you decide how much risk to take and how hard to push yourself.

You can use the exercise at the end of the chapter to help you recognize the changes in your moods and how they affect your sense of self and your ability to interact with other people.

Getting Stuck in Your Thoughts and Moods

When you have BSD, you not only are more prone to intense emotions (either positive or negative), but you may also be less flexible in your emotional responses. You may have a more difficult time shifting attention away from thoughts that are accompanied by strong feelings.

Part of the problem is that BSD undermines your ability to regulate the physical responses you have when experiencing emotions. When you have a strong negative emotion, you can sometimes feel your heart race or your muscles tense. You see the signs that your body is ready for action. You hyperfocus your attention, locking it on whatever the danger is. A branch of the nervous system called the sympathetic branch is responsible for getting us ready for "fight or flight." This activation is helpful in times of crisis.

But people with BSD can find it difficult to shift their attention and slow down when they get too activated. The branch of the nervous system called the parasympathetic branch has the role of slowing us down when our thoughts race too much. New research is showing that our ability to flexibly shift our attention is related to the activity of our parasympathetic nervous system. When we are physically more relaxed, we can get our mind off of difficult topics.

What Is the Bottom Line?

The most important thing is to recognize that the difficulties you have getting started on your work or being with other people may really be symptoms of mood-regulation problems. At first you may think you have a problem with procrastination, intelligence, or passion. Sometimes Sonja thinks she is just lazy or not smart enough to handle her schoolwork. Gene thinks he is mysteriously self-defeating, probably because of some problems in his childhood. Lucia thinks she is just too sensitive. But it may be more accurate and helpful to recognize that at least part of these problems reflect difficulties in mood regulation.

If you suspect that your difficulties are really mood-regulation symptoms, it's time to talk to your doctor. It may be important to get your medication adjusted so that these mood symptoms are at a minimum. Often doctors will use mood-stabilizing medications to help you tolerate your moods. Other times the addition of antipsychotics (such as Risperdal or Seroquel) can slow down racing thoughts and make you a little more thick skinned. Occasionally, it can be helpful to carefully consider antidepressants or antianxiety medications.

For example, adding a small dose of a mood stabilizer (lithium) did the trick for both Gene and Sonja. The medication stabilized Sonja's mood, so her thinking could proceed without so many mood-related interruptions. She could finish her thoughts and ideas. As her mood stabilized, Sonja made an outline of her assignments, and she was better able to organize her paper. For Gene, decreasing his antidepressant and increasing his mood stabilizer helped him contain his excitement and slow the racing thoughts. Gene was more effective in his creativity now. He could take his ideas and work them all the way through, instead of just experiencing them dancing around in his brain. For Lucia, adding a small dose of an antipsychotic to her current regimen of mood-stabilizing medications made a world of difference. She could be around other people with much greater ease.

It may take some time to achieve a medication regimen that slows down your thoughts without slowing them down too much. You don't want to feel too flat and constricted. It can be necessary to readjust the medications or dosages several times, because these symptoms can change as your life changes.

Behavioral Strategies

You can also use behavioral strategies that reduce your agitation. This can include whatever strategies help you slow down, including exercise, meditation, yoga, prayer, and social support to help you become more flexible in your thinking. These techniques can support your independence.

For example, we taught Aviva, a patient with bipolar disorder and OCD, some relaxation exercises. One technique called autogenic training, developed by Johannes Schultz and Wolfgang Luthe, essentially provides instruction in relaxing or regulating your physical state. This involves repeating the self-hypnosis sentences in a chant. Aviva would chant, "My arms and legs are heavy and warm, my breathing is deep and slow, my heartbeat is slow and steady, and I am calm and peaceful."

Sometimes when Aviva is in a mixed state, she will get stuck in an obsessive loop, thinking repetitive thoughts about physical illness. At these times I encourage her to start chanting to calm herself down. I will chant with her on the phone (or her grandmother will chant with her at home) until she is calm enough to turn her attention away from these scary thoughts.

For other people, having someone nearby—a friend or family member—can calm their agitation and help stabilize their mood, at least for a short while.

EXERCISE 10
Mood Lability Chart

One of the most difficult aspects of BSD is that your memories of the way you feel and the way you feel about yourself change as your mood changes. So mood lability can change your sense of your own personal history. It can be helpful to keep track of your moods and the ways they affect your feelings about yourself. When you feel bad, it can be useful to know that you have had periods when you felt well. And when you feel upset and angry with someone, it can be helpful to know that things didn't always feel that way. In this chart you can keep track of the ways your moods change and how they affect your thoughts about yourself and your ability to be with others. If you are already tracking your symptoms on the table for Exercise 6, you can just add a column there for your thoughts. You might want to pick a regularly scheduled day a week when you spend a few minutes tracking the way you feel—for example, every Thursday evening before you watch a particular show on TV. Then you take a minute to note your mood and your thoughts about yourself and your feelings about one person who is close to you. You don't need to tell them what you are thinking; you are just keeping track of your feelings. You will see changes in the way you think as your mood changes. You can add more entries if you see a big mood change, but it's always helpful to have a regular time for tracking. Our patients find it helpful when we point out the ways their feelings have changed over time and how their thoughts shift with their moods.

Here's an example:

Date	Your Mood Right Now (e.g., irritable, sad, relaxed, happy, anxious)	Your Thoughts About Yourself	Your Social Activities (times you were with other people and how you felt)
Sept. 3, 2007	Irritable	"I never get anything done. Other people always interrupt me. It drives me crazy."	"Saw my sister, felt comfortable. Didn't socialize with anyone else."
Sept. 10, 2007	Relaxed	"I feel OK about how things are going."	"Was able to go to a volunteer activity at the kids' school. Saw a friend for lunch. Saw my sister later."

Now it's your turn:

Date	Your Mood Right Now (e.g., irritable, sad, relaxed, happy, anxious)	Your Thoughts About Yourself	Your Social Activities (times you were with other people and how you felt)

Date	Your Mood Right Now (e.g., irritable, sad, relaxed, happy, anxious)	Your Thoughts About Yourself	Your Social Activities (times you were with other people and how you felt)

Notes for the Family

What looks like racing thoughts to you won't necessarily feel like racing thoughts to your family member with BSD. In fact, these thoughts may feel particularly important or interesting. Or the person may feel confident and smart for the first time in his or her life.

It may be very difficult to tell someone that you are worried about the way they are talking or acting or that their thinking does not really make complete sense. If this person already has a doctor, you may be in luck, because you can call the doctor and discuss these issues.

If this is the first time your loved one is having symptoms, and you are just beginning to suspect that he or she has a BSD, the situation may be more difficult. You will need patience to work this through. There is probably no easy way to tell someone that you are worried he or she feels too elated and is having too many ideas, no easy way to say, "We are worried that you are actually sick, even though you have never felt better"—especially because people in this state are often irritable. You can sometimes get assistance from your own doctor. You can sometimes use a low-key approach. It is good to have multiple options and multiple resources and to use each one as it is appropriate.

It can be harder to think about recovery from bipolar disorder in the same way you think about recovery from a physical ailment—you can actually see the recovery as someone learns to walk again. But the same process takes place as people recover from BSD. You just have to learn to look for it.

I Thought I Was Smart, but I Just Can't Perform

The Role of Information-Processing Problems

KEY POINTS

BSD is associated with specific information-processing problems, including difficulties in working and declarative memory.

These information-processing problems can make small tasks feel very difficult and can make it hard to learn new information.

Information-processing problems can also affect social relationships.

Understanding these difficulties can help you structure tasks to make them easier.

Neuropsychologists conduct studies to evaluate the cognitive (or thinking) difficulties of people with bipolar disorder. As we have discussed in Chapter 4, many studies have reported that people with BSD show significant problems with attention, concentration, and working memory. You can also think of working memory as a kind of "mental space" for immediate information processing. Problems in several different brain structures can limit the amount of space you have available for tasks such as taking in new information, translating it into your own words, fitting it into your existing knowledge, and retrieving it when you need it. Problems in working memory are also sometimes accompanied by problems in planning and organization. (Some of these difficulties are the reason that BSD can be misdiagnosed as ADD.)

"Why Don't I Feel as Smart as I Used To?"

These problems affect your ability to master new or unfamiliar material. They do not necessarily affect your basic intelligence or your ability to understand ideas, to draw conclusions, or to appreciate art or music. But because most people are not neuropsychologists, they don't have a good way to think about thinking. They have a tendency to see all of their mental abilities as one. That's why you can feel you are getting "dumber and dumber," as one patient put it, or why you can wonder about your motivation when you don't succeed at certain tasks. Problems in working memory can create significant problems in functioning, but they don't mean people are dumb or unmotivated.

There is some evidence that problems in working memory and certain other cognitive functions may be present even before the first mood symptoms of BSD emerge. Studies show that adolescents who are at risk for BSD (because a parent has the condition) display some of these symptoms, even when the adolescents have not shown traditional mood-related symptoms of BSD themselves.

Most research has suggested that these problems in working memory or other types of information processing are worse when you are acutely ill—depressed or manic. However, recent research suggests that there may be some problems that remain even when you are feeling reasonably well. Clinically, it is our experience that many, although not all, of these problems resolve when the patient achieves consistent mood stability. And things continue to get better the longer the mood is stable.

People will vary in the degree to which these information-processing problems are present. Some will have minimal problems, while others will have more serious difficulties. There is some evidence that these problems are worse for people who are depressed or when they are depressed. But the problems can be present in hypomania as well. Working memory problems are made worse by stress (and that's true for everyone). But stress-related difficulties in information processing may be particularly problematic for people who have BSD.

Problems with working memory affect a wide variety of activities, from studying to talking on the phone. Let's look at a few examples to see how working memory problems can make life more difficult—and to generate some ideas for getting around these problems.

Kate's Story

Let's look at the reasons why Kate, one of our examples from Chapter 8, was having so much trouble in school. She had tremendous difficulty doing the required reading and paying attention in class. When she should have been taking notes in lectures, she found she couldn't remember or process what the professor had said long enough to commit it to paper. When she should have been studying, she was reading the newspaper.

Kate came to see me with all kinds of questions about her motivation: "Maybe I don't really like school." "Maybe I'm not really smart enough." "Maybe I am really lazy." "Maybe I don't really want to be an investment banker." She had all sorts of psychological and sociological explanations for her behavior. She just knew that if she were motivated, she would have done well.

And if you met Kate, you would see she is a very smart and interesting person. You wouldn't think there was anything wrong with her thinking.

But Kate "forgot" that she has bipolar disorder. After more serious problems, she had stabilized on her medication and been doing well for several years. She had some ups and downs, but they didn't interfere with her ability to go to work. She generally did better after a day off or a change in medication.

Business school was a major change in stress and a major change in the amount of information she had to absorb and manage at any one time. When she was working, before she went to business school, she could pace herself. Her job at an investment company involved some very challenging activities as well as some pretty boring repetitive tasks.

When she felt overwhelmed or couldn't concentrate, she focused on the boring administrative tasks. As she put it, "There's nothing like stuffing envelopes for a few hours to help you calm down." When she felt better or when there was a team meeting where she could get encouraged by the companionship of her coworkers and supervisors, she could do more complex and challenging tasks.

When the Demand for Concentration Is High. Working hard in business school requires a different approach. You can take quick breaks from studying, but for the most part, you need to concentrate for long periods. Kate needed to stay on task and independently push herself to read very complicated material.

Just like Kate, when you are studying, you need to be able to put the sentences from the book into your mind, translate them into your own words, match them to your existing understanding of the information, and adjust your understanding to respond to the new information. If the information is very complicated and is pretty unfamiliar, it takes up more "space" in your mind.

For example, if you already understand a lot about a topic—say, baseball—and you are reading about a game in the sports section of the day's paper, you'll find it easy to remember all the information. You have a context for understanding the information given in the newspaper story. You know who the teams and players are, you understand what statistics are important to remember, and you have an idea about game strategy. You understand what the writer is describing when he writes about the plays that won the game. You memorize the scores and the actions of the key players without even thinking about it. The information just slides into place.

But if you knew nothing about the game or the teams, reading that story would take a lot more work. The names of the teams and the players would be unfamiliar; you would have to work to remember them. You'd probably have to come up with some kind of mental strategy to keep all those players in mind. You might not understand the writer's descriptions of the game, and you would have to reread the story several times to get the details down.

So when Kate said she couldn't take notes in class, she was right. It wasn't that she was unmotivated—she just really couldn't do it under those conditions. She heard the words the professor spoke, but she couldn't retain enough of the information in her working memory to be able to translate them into more familiar concepts and fit them into her existing knowledge about the way finance works.

Revisiting the Effort Scale. Before she got sick, a difficult class, like calculus, might have taken about a 5 on the effort scale that we examined in Chapter 6. When she wasn't sick, with a little extra effort and big desire to get an A, she could force herself to concentrate. New information always requires extra effort to process (you have to generate new contexts or stories to guide your understanding of the details). After Kate got sick, a hard class demanded much more effort than she could muster—maybe even more than a 10.

If she did a little each day for each class, she would never catch up. And she was afraid that by the time she had mastered one new piece of information, she would have forgotten the old material. Her feelings of being overwhelmed intensified the problem. And the guilt and shame she felt as she read the newspaper knowing all her classmates were busy studying made things even worse.

It is important to note that Kate realizes she is very intelligent. That just makes it worse for her. Because she didn't know about working memory and BSD, she couldn't understand why someone as smart as she is couldn't master the material. She thought, "It just has to be a problem with motivation."

Breaking Down the Problem and Building Up Your Supports

Problems with working memory can make it very difficult to get things done. And because you are generally not aware of the different ways your mind works, you don't realize that these are problems with working memory. You just know that you are having trouble with new information. You see that it is difficult to develop systematic ways of solving problems.

How can you combat some of these difficulties? The first step involves asking yourself some questions: "Am I having problems getting started because I am having difficulty organizing my approach to the job?" "Can I break down the job into smaller parts?" This is called task analysis.

Task Analysis

In the past, you might have been able to do task analysis automatically. You might think, "Ugh, I don't like paying the bills, but if I just get all the envelopes together and line them up and pull out the checkbook, it will get done." This automatic task analysis—breaking down the task into its parts—just doesn't happen without effort for some people with bipolar disorder.

When people with bipolar disorder try to break a task down, they can do it, but it takes more effort than before. This task analysis requires executive functioning (see Chapter 4), in that it uses the part of your brain that is analytic and very systematic. It also requires that you inhibit or turn off your emotional reaction to each thought. That can be a hard thing to do when you have BSD. But it isn't impossible when you are less anxious.

Why is it important to break the task down? You want to break the task down into little parts that require only a modest amount of effort. If you can break the job down into a task that you can "just *do*" without really thinking much about it, you can trick the BSD. When it isn't very hard to do a chore, most people will do it. When the chores are more difficult, most people have to be much more motivated to get them done.

Pamela's Story. Let's look at another example. Pamela was enrolled in a biology class. She was just starting back at school after being very ill, so she was taking just one course. She knew she was not yet ready to handle the stress of a full load, but even when taking only one course, she still felt overwhelmed by all the material. She just couldn't think of a strategy for studying. She wanted to understand everything at once but felt like she couldn't make anything stick in her head. She called me in a frantic state, because she had a test later that week and didn't see how she could learn all the material. I asked her to bring her textbooks to the session.

Pamela was having difficulty because she has some problems with working memory and other problems with executive function. She just wasn't ready to organize the task on her own. So together we broke down the task of studying into smaller pieces. I asked

Pamela to write down a chapter's vocabulary words on index cards. She knew she could do that—it doesn't take much concentration. (In effect, her hands were doing the work.) After she finished, I asked her to write the definitions on the back of the first five cards. She got to work. Again this was a structured task, one she could do. When she was done, we worked on the next five cards. Within forty-five minutes, Pamela had created a set of cards to study from, and she had calmed herself down.

Pamela wasn't yet able to organize the task herself, but she could do the studying if she was given some structure. The knowledge went into her head without much effort as she wrote the definitions on the cards. (It's worth noting that Pamela is now able to organize herself.)

In Exercise 11, at the end of the chapter, you can take a difficult task you are facing and perform a task analysis to break it into more manageable parts. List all parts of the task. Keep breaking the parts further down until you have activities that you rate as requiring a level 4 effort. (Not what you think other people will rate as a level 4, but what *you* really rate as a level 4.)

Most people will do things that require (for them) about a level 4 effort or less but need more motivation to try something harder. The score assigned to any task will be different for each person. It depends on your level of experience and your anxiety. This may seem like a tedious process, but it can really be helpful. Once this becomes second nature for you, you will be better able to accomplish your goals.

Working Memory and Interpersonal Relationships

Working memory problems can also affect your willingness to interact with other people. Sometimes people can't tolerate conversations or other interactions because they may intuitively sense they won't be able to process the information fast enough. This may be what drives one of the most common symptoms of bipolar—telephone phobia. No, people are not afraid of the telephone, but they are apprehensive and nervous about having to talk to people on the telephone. And they end up avoiding many activities, they avoid scheduling events, or they avoid clarifying information because they are afraid to talk on the phone. Again, this is a double-edged sword, because oftentimes people with BSD will feel immediate relief from a particularly bothersome symptom if they were able to pick up a phone and call their doctor or a loved one.

Pamela's Problems with Phone Calls

Let's look at an example. Pamela was having problems with her Internet service. She could not get her phone and the Internet to work at the same time, as it was supposed to. I suggested she call the technical support service to get a clearer idea on how to do this.

Pamela refused. She absolutely hates to talk on the phone. She really cannot manage it. She gets too rattled and will not use the phone to make calls to get information or change plans, unless she really has to do it.

Why? Talking on the phone requires some of the same working memory abilities that make studying so hard for her. But at least when she is at home in front of a book and on her own, she does not have to think at the pace directed by the other person. She can move as slowly as she needs to, repeating and reviewing the information when she gets distracted. And no one is watching her struggle.

But on the phone, she can't escape. She really can't avoid the puzzlement or disapproval of the other person. And she has some pride in herself, so it is hard to tolerate having other people think she is stupid or dazed when she is talking on the phone. The pace of a phone call is just too fast. (Not too fast for intellectual discussions, but too fast for problem solving in an unfamiliar area.)

Why Are Phone Calls So Hard?

Many people with bipolar can talk about personal things or can listen to others, but they have much more difficulty when learning new information or resolving technical problems over the phone (technical problems can include getting directions, changing appointments, understanding how to fix an insurance problem, and so on).

And if it is a call about an anxiety-producing topic, things can get worse. When people feel as if they are in a dangerous situation, their fear can make their information-processing abilities worse, not better. Here's one way to think about what this can feel like. If you were in the middle of the jungle being chased by a tiger, you just wouldn't expect to be able to learn French from your iPod at the same time. And you wouldn't even expect to be able to learn French for a while after the jungle experience. You might not even expect to be able to use the iPod. You would know intuitively that all that excitement makes it hard to concentrate and take in the information you are receiving. During these calls, Pamela's body is giving her the same messages as if she were running through the jungle away from a tiger.

It is humiliating to have so much difficulty talking on the phone. There is also the fear that people can see how impaired you are—that your brain dysfunction is suddenly on view as if your skull were made of glass and other people could see how mixed up and confused you feel. And people with BSD can feel angry and frustrated about how hard this is and make up excuses or complicated psychological reasons why they are afraid.

Family members get frustrated and angry as well and can make things worse when they see this problem as a simple problem of character or anxiety. They can push too hard, and that pushing increases the anxiety. For example, Pamela has to face some criticism and frustration from her parents and friends when they interpret her behavior as a character or anxiety problem: "That Pamela never takes care of anything." "Pamela doesn't really want to take care of herself, she is lazy and dependent."

Is she lazy or dependent or avoidant? No, it's just that the information-processing demands are a little overwhelming. Let's examine it bit by bit. A telephone call to get help involves lots of different sentences, one after the other.

The first sentence might be OK: "Hi, this is Pamela, and I wanted some help getting my Internet service to work." She can practice that sentence and get it out. But life gets more complicated from then on in. The technical support person may ask her to describe the problem. She can probably do that, because she has been talking about it with her family and friends. But the next several sentences are much less predictable. If the technical support person asks her questions about how things worked before and what she has done to fix the problem, Pamela will have difficulty.

These kinds of conversations can be confusing and difficult for many people. But the difficulty for Pamela is that she cannot quickly integrate the new information with her existing knowledge. She really has to concentrate. She feels as if the new sentences are just flying by, like sticks in a river, instead of assembling and building up a sturdy structure. She sees all these sentences carried by the current, and she feels more and more panicked as they float downstream away from her understanding.

How You Can Make Talking a Little Easier

To make telephoning a little easier, you may want to try Exercise 11 to break down the conversation and try to anticipate what information will be required. This makes the conversation more predictable and controllable. In Pamela's case, she can create a context for the new information. This helps her store the information and then retrieve it. She is not trying to understand the facts and think about what to do both at the same time. Instead, she has some ideas in advance. So, for example, we think through various options for what the technical support person might say. We try to write down the steps in the conversation, including her first few sentences (introduction and sentences about the problems). She can keep this in front of her when she makes the call.

Sometimes I have Pamela make the calls from my office. The social support and the knowledge that I will move her past any difficulties keep her calmer. And that calmness helps her stay focused and less distracted. She is still pretty shaky, but her heart is less likely to race. By minimizing stress, we prevent the stress hormones from interfering with her ability to store information, and this will make her memories of the conversation less foggy. So it is helpful to take on these tasks when you can have some support.

Learning to Ask for Help and to Move On

Ultimately, we came to realize that the informational demands of many, but not all, kinds of conversations are simply too hard for Pamela at this point. So she will make the ones she can, forgive herself for the ones that are too hard, and explain the situation to her family in a more straightforward way. Once they understood, they all agreed it was simply easier and more efficient for different family members to make some of the calls. When her family understood more about the nature of the burden, they were more willing and less resentful about taking on the responsibility. And Pamela is less ashamed and more willing to do more. She does better when she chooses tasks that she can succeed at without exhausting herself.

Keeping Track of Successes

Many people with BSD-related information-processing problems have difficulty learning from their positive experiences. That's why

Pamela often asks, "Why can't I just realize that my experience was OK and use that knowledge to help me the next time?" She continues to anticipate difficulty, because she can't yet trust her mind to think. So contrary to the way you might treat "phone phobia" if it were just an anxiety disorder, pushing your way past the fear, it might be better to use a different approach, a calming approach that builds on successive accomplishments.

Because these calls are very challenging, it can be hard to see if you are making progress. You may have difficulty with this task for a long time. And because it is something that seems so easy for other people (and may have been so easy for you before you got sick), you can still feel angry and disappointed even when you are making steady progress but are not perfectly able to handle conversations.

It is worth keeping track of gains. For example, when she first started treatment, Pamela could not make any calls. Gradually she began to make smaller calls, scheduling appointments or ordering tickets. As time went on (and it is worth understanding that it was a lot of time), she began to be able to order things on the phone, handling a series of questions about preferences. Now she still hates it, but she can make brief calls to her pharmacy and insurance company to try to solve problems. These kinds of calls require that Pamela quickly process information in real time and adjust her answers depending on what the operator says.

It may be helpful for you to realize which kinds of conversations you can have on the phone and which kinds are hard. Exercise 12 at the end of this chapter includes a chart to help you keep track of the kinds of calls you can make. Use the chart to score how much stress you feel when making these different kinds of calls. Keep a copy of this chart, and notice how you are doing six months from now. Tell your doctor. You can use this kind of analysis to help you understand how your treatment is affecting one aspect of your working memory.

Notes for the Family

These information-processing problems can be the most disabling part of BSD, and they can be the most confusing. When people don't seem to want to function, it can be confusing. You may wonder if it is illness or a character problem (such as cowardice, laziness, or selfishness). You wonder if you should push the person.

If your family member had an anxiety disorder without BSD, it would be appropriate to push him or her to take risks and get going. In BSD the issues are not so clear. You really wouldn't push someone to do something that was beyond his or her capability. You might help your loved one to break the task down and lend support for whatever he or she can do independently.

Because this is such a gray area, you are in the position of deciding if something is possible but difficult and a little push will help—or if it is impossible and you should provide assistance instead.

It is important to talk through the information-processing demands. You can ask your family member questions about why something is too hard. These conversations may not go easily.

First, you can try to think about what is required to do the task—what kinds of concentration and attention are needed. Then you can either provide some assistance (without discussion) or you can talk it through with your family member. As you can imagine, it is very alarming and humiliating for a person to realize that thinking things through is so hard.

It may be that a soft and quiet discussion about the demands of the situation will help. You can figure out what support or help the person needs. For example, a common problem is that people with working memory problems hate to make telephone calls to get information or make reservations. It may be helpful to work with your family member to come up with ways to help make certain calls (e.g., to stay in the room, to write down a script, etc.).

It can be helpful to keep track of the progress. Things will get better as mood stabilizes. Most people with working memory difficulties only focus on how much they can't do and feel they have lost. So even when they are regaining function, they can feel as if they are still disabled. You might want to keep track of the kinds of progress your loved one has made—note which calls he or she can make alone, which events he or she can plan, which chores or work responsibilities he or she can complete. (It may help for you to fill out some of the worksheets in the back of this chapter as well.)

EXERCISE 11
Breaking Down a Difficult Task

Remember Angela from Chapter 6? Here is an example of a task analysis we did to help her work through some of her paperwork—in particular, filing her medical insurance claims.

Activity	Effort Score (on a scale of 1 to 10)	Why Is It Hard?	What Steps Need to Be Taken to Get It Done?
Get the bills together in one pile on the desk	3	"I am afraid I won't be able to find all the bills." "I am ashamed that I have procrastinated so long." "I am afraid that if I can't find them on my desk, I won't know where to look."	"I'll break this task into two parts: first, get together just the bills in the biggest pile on my desk. Then I'll find the other bills."
Open the envelopes	2	"I think I can do this. I am a little afraid about what I might see in the bills, but I can at least open them and lay them out."	"Just do it."
Get out the insurance forms and attach the bills to the forms	2	"I think I can do this, too. I may be anxious finding the forms in my drawer, but I'll keep looking."	"I will put the forms on the table one day and leave them there to work on the next day, so they are easily available."

Activity	Effort Score (on a scale of 1 to 10)	Why Is It Hard?	What Steps Need to Be Taken to Get It Done?
Write in the information on the insurance forms	4	"I get very anxious about making a mistake."	"I can do it and then see if they send it back to me. Or I can have someone else look it over."
Put the forms in the envelopes	4	"I wonder if I have the right address."	"I will do it."

Now pick a task that is difficult for you to do. Break the task down into little steps, each of which is no harder than a 4. Go back and revisit the goals and steps each week. How did you do? Mark the things that you accomplish. Think about the things you still have trouble doing. Decide if you need to break any steps down into smaller pieces.

Activity	Effort Score (on a scale of 1 to 10)	Why Is It Hard?	What Steps Need to Be Taken to Get It Done?	Did It Get Done? (if not, break it down further)

You can also use the same strategies to make a to-do list for the week. Don't overload the list. Try to improve your ability to make your actions meet your intentions. See if you can really do the things on your urgent list. And try to figure out how long each task will take you. This will help you break the cycle, because you will get better able to predict what you can do and what you should expect each week. Most important, these task lists can help you structure your day. And this structure is key to helping you stabilize your mood and get your symptoms under better control.

Task list for the week of ....

Urgent	Less Urgent but Still Important	If You Can Get to It

EXERCISE 12
Keeping Track of Progress

Here is a special worksheet for keeping track of your progress making telephone calls.

Your phone call progress for the week of _____

Kinds of Telephone Calls	Do You Make These Kinds of Calls?	How Much Effort Will It Take to Make This Call? (on a scale of 1 to 10)	Is the Conversation Likely to Involve a Conflict—to Become Emotional or Argumentative?	Will You Need to Understand New Information? (yes or no)	Do You Need to Make Decisions?	Did You Make the Calls?
Making an appointment with a familiar doctor						
Calling a friend to hear about how he or she is doing						
Ordering take-out food						
Calling a repair service to get help						

Kinds of Telephone Calls	Do You Make These Kinds of Calls?	How Much Effort Will It Take to Make This Call? (on a scale of 1 to 10)	Is the Conversation Likely to Involve a Conflict—to Become Emotional or Argumentative?	Will You Need to Understand New Information? (yes or no)	Do You Need to Make Decisions?	Did You Make the Calls?
Calling to correct a billing error						
Calling to complain about a mistake						
Calling to make reservations						
Calling to find out information						
Calling a doctor to ask for information or help						
Calling a store, movie theater, or museum to ask a question about hours or schedules						

Kinds of Telephone Calls	Do You Make These Kinds of Calls?	How Much Effort Will It Take to Make This Call? (on a scale of 1 to 10)	Is the Conversation Likely to Involve a Conflict—to Become Emotional or Argumentative?	Will You Need to Understand New Information? (yes or no)	Do You Need to Make Decisions?	Did You Make the Calls?
Calling to solve a problem in the house						
Calling to work things out with a friend or relative after a dispute						
Calling to ask someone to help you						
Add your own types of calls:						

Just When I Felt OK, I Got Sick Again

The Dangers of Relapse

KEY POINTS

A variety of factors can influence relapse.

You may see seasonal changes in your mood and functioning.

BSD affects your ability to tolerate stress.

Even minor stressors can cause big shifts in mood.

Daily structure can help you buffer stress and control the cycling.

Recognizing the early warning signs of stress can help you break the bipolar cycle.

One of the most difficult problems facing people with bipolar disorder is the unpredictable nature of the condition. Just when you feel like you might be getting better, you get sick again. Maybe you get depressed; maybe you get manic or hypomanic. This makes it hard to maintain your morale, to feel confident about taking risks, to think about going back to work, or to feel as if you will ever be well again.

The difficulty is that these relapses can seem unpredictable and uncontrollable. And when events seem unpredictable or uncontrollable, they can seem very dangerous and threatening. A relapse, even a minor one, can leave you feeling hopeless and frightened and very angry. These feelings can make the situation worse. Relapses are also frustrating, anxiety producing, and dispiriting to those who care about you. Sometimes if your friends and family cannot understand what is happening, they start to feel as if you aren't trying to get better or as if you are hopelessly ill.

But it isn't necessary to get so catastrophic. These relapses are not as unpredictable or uncontrollable as they seem. You can understand the factors that lead to these changes, if you are thoughtful about keeping track of your experiences.

Some relapses may be related to seasonal changes in mood. Other relapses may be related to increases in stress, even low levels of stress. Finally, as we discussed in Chapter 5, changes in medication can also trigger mood changes.

Seasons and Weather

The evidence linking changes in seasons or weather to symptom changes in bipolar disorder is mixed, but it is likely to be the case that at least some people experience changes in mood as the seasons change. Changes in the amount of daylight (or even the angle at which the sun's rays hit the earth) can trigger changes in our internal clock. These changes can affect the daily cycles of our neurohormones and affect the way we feel (see Chapter 4, on neurobiology).

When the seasons change you won't necessarily have a relapse; you just may be more sensitive to stress. For example, one of our patients, John, often has mood-regulation difficulties in April. Two years ago, his wife went back to work in April, leaving John on his own most of the day. The year she went back to work, John got very sick for several weeks. The next year, he had some symptoms during the early spring, but he was able to make it through this time period without losing more than a day of work. In his case, it's likely that the combination of the stress of his wife going back to work and the seasonal changes was associated with more symptoms than either a stressful event or a seasonal change alone. As people recover, in general they seem better able to handle the seasonal changes in mood regulation.

You can keep track of seasonal changes in symptoms yourself. Try to remember if you always used to feel bad at any particular time of the year—perhaps during summer vacation, as school started, or over the December holidays. Many people have difficulty in late September or October, around the fall equinox. This is often a time when people become more depressed. Another difficult time is March–April, around the time of the spring equinox. This is likely to be a time of increase in hypomanic or mixed-state symptoms. April is the month in which people are more likely to commit suicide than any other month in the year. So it is worth paying attention and getting help if you feel bad at these times.

You can make brief notes on your mood and energy throughout the year and notice any patterns. You can use a calendar to record your mood, energy level, and sleep patterns. This can help you get prepared for any seasonal fluctuations in mood. You can anticipate needing to reduce your stress level and potentially make medication changes or increase your social support. It's worth noting that you may have an anniversary reaction, an increase in symptoms, during the season you first got sick or were hospitalized.

Stress

Bipolar disorder is a stress-related disorder. BSD isn't caused by stress, but the symptoms of BSD make you more sensitive to stress, and increased levels of stress can inflame your symptoms. Problems with mood regulation make it hard to manage your emotional reactions to stressors. Problems with information processing make it hard to develop and follow through on reasonable plans to cope with these stressors. In turn, stress can increase your symptoms and affect your ability to recover.

How does this work? You may remember that we talked in Chapter 4 about how the hormones released when you are stressed (for example, norepinephrine and cortisol) influence cell signaling and other physical responses throughout your body. This cascade of physical changes can undermine your stamina and make it much harder for you to recover from small episodes of stress.

The good news is that this will get better. As you stabilize your mood you will get much more resilient in response to stress. Effective stress management can help, and it starts with an understanding of the ways events can trigger stress reactions.

We can use research from stress and coping theory to help guide our understanding of these relapses. Let's think about what *stress* means. Every situation or event makes some demands on us—emotional, intellectual, or physical. We experience these demands as stressful when we think they exceed our capacity to cope or make us doubt our knowledge about ourselves.

When BSD strikes, your old self-knowledge isn't really accurate. There are significant changes in the things you will perceive as stressful. Even minor events can trigger symptoms, and everyday chores can seem very stressful. It can seem impossible to call the pharmacy to fix a problem with a prescription or to make dinner or help with homework. Handling an interpersonal conflict at work—even minor teasing around the watercooler—can seem like an overwhelming battle.

Why are these little tasks so stressful? They are more stressful because you have some changes in your ability to cope; these changes are largely a function of difficulties with information processing and mood regulation, and they may also be affected by changes in your physical stamina. Situations can also be more stressful because you are just less familiar with your ability to cope. If you don't fully understand the effects of BSD on your mood, thinking, and behavior, your difficulties take you by surprise. And they will keep taking you by surprise if you don't realize how the BSD changes the perception of stress.

Your Ability to Cope with Stress

Let's look at the initial changes in your coping capacity. Both BSD and the medications for BSD can affect your memory. You may feel like you are not able to think as well as you used to, so it can be a little more difficult to maintain your concentration or work through a complex problem. And BSD certainly makes your emotions more intense and less controllable. Consequently, you may not know if you will be able to think clearly or keep your mood in control. You may be physically more tired, because the medicine may be sedating you, managing your symptoms is exhausting, and often your sleep is disturbed. You may feel physically weaker or less coordinated, because some medicines interfere with your balance and fine motor skills.

Many of these problems will improve with good treatment. But as you are recovering, you need to learn how these difficulties (symptoms and side effects) might affect your coping ability. You need to learn how you will react under different circumstances. Most events will seem stressful if you don't know how you will react, how you will handle the challenges. Think about your first job or first date (or first root canal)—those situations were much scarier because they were unfamiliar.

When you don't know how you will react and can't count on your capacities, you are less able to predict and then control your responses. This uncertainty can be painful and alarming. And if you overdo it, refuse to slow down to accommodate the changes, you will get sicker. You will have more bipolar cycles.

Let's just do the math. If you are a weight lifter with lots of big, strong muscles and experience bench-pressing two hundred pounds of metal, you might not view the requirement to lift a fifty-pound weight as very stressful. In fact, you might not need any concentration or effort at all. Fifty pounds is only a quarter of what you usually lift—it's easy. No stress at all. On the other hand, a middle-aged woman who struggles to bench-press thirty-five pounds would view the requirement to lift fifty pounds as pretty stressful. She might be able to do it, but she would really have to concentrate and certainly couldn't keep it up for long. She just wouldn't have the muscle power to do it. And fifty pounds is a lot heavier than she would be used to. In fact, it is 143 percent of her usual workload. Is she going to think that those same fifty pounds are stressful? Yes!

If your coping capacity has changed, events that seemed like no big deal before may seem very stressful. It takes some time to get used to the changes in your internal state to understand that your reactions are different. It is a significant loss to see your coping resources undermined. You need time to get the medications straightened out to help stabilize your mood, and you need time to learn what you can and can't tolerate.

Marisol's Story. Let's look at an example. Marisol was feeling much better after a manic episode in which she became psychotic and had to be hospitalized. She was now out of the hospital, resuming some regular activities, and thinking about what the next step should be. About eight weeks after the hospitalization, however, she began feeling more anxious. She couldn't sleep through the night, and any social contact felt overwhelming.

What happened? Marisol said nothing really happened to make her symptoms worse. There were no big events; nothing so important really happened to cause her to feel so stressed. In fact, people with BSD often say, "I had a relapse, but nothing really happened to cause it. There were no breakups, no job loss, or anything else. What is going on?" But what they really mean is, "No event happened that I would have considered stressful before I got sick."

When Marisol came out of the hospital, she returned to school. She was taking one class. The relapse after the eighth week coincided with the approach of midterm exams. She knew she felt anxious about the midterm, but she was surprised that she was having so much trouble.

Before she got sick, tests and papers would make her feel about a 5 on the stress scale. But her mood-regulation and information-processing symptoms made the exam feel more like a 10. Her difficulties with concentration make her feel she has to spend more time studying, and her mood-regulation problems mean that she has to take more time to recover when she gets anxious or has a difficult day.

Once she recognized how the disorder was making the situation more stressful, she understood that she needed to take even small stressors a little more seriously. Now she plans to rest before and after the final exam. It was painful, but she decided to accept that she just needs a little extra time to recover. She realized her relapse meant that she has to take it a little easier when there are increases in class demands, even if those increases wouldn't have seemed important to her before she got sick. This gave her a greater sense of control.

As Marisol has been pacing herself, she has gotten much better. She recognizes the signs of stress at an earlier stage and adjusts her activity level to compensate. Consequently, she is not experiencing very big ups and downs. Her concentration has substantially improved. She is taking more courses and is applying to graduate school. She feels as if she can better predict how to live to accommodate the BSD and still move forward with her life.

Marisol had been sick with a very painful medical problem about five years earlier. When she got sick, she learned she absolutely had to take it easy or she would really be in pain and incapacitated. And she decided that she would take the medicines the doctors offered her, even though they gave her some troubling side effects. Marisol told me that she thought that the experience she had adjusting to her first illness helped her adjust more rapidly to the BSD.

Ava's Story. But it can be really difficult to face the fact that you have to adjust your expectations to accommodate your current difficulties. Ava, who has bipolar II, is about to return to work. After being out of full-time work for more than a year as she recovered, Ava is going to take a new full-time job. During the course of her initial recovery, she took on some part-time work to help her get back on her feet and get used to her condition, to help her understand and predict how she would react under different circumstances. She was very upset at having to work part time and felt humiliated and angered by her limitations. But these jobs helped her develop new coping and stress-management skills. Now that she is going to full-time work, we talk about what the first few weeks will be like.

Ava said that she wanted to take some classes after work. I told Ava that it had been my experience that starting a new job (or really almost any new activity) was often very stressful for people with BSD—stressful in ways they just couldn't always anticipate. It might be better for her to plan that, in the beginning, she would just come home and rest after work.

She got really angry and upset. "The medications make me sleep so long—ten to twelve hours. My whole life will be work and sleep. Why do I have to do that? Why can't I have a life? I used to be able to go to work, take classes, go out in the evenings, and run around as much as I wanted. Why do I have to act like an invalid? If I have to rest, then I am accepting that I am damaged and sick. Why should I accept that?"

There are no easy answers to these questions. We have never had a patient who didn't express these same feelings at some point (or at many points). The problem is that if you don't accept that you have had changes in your ability to tolerate stress, you are more likely to overwhelm yourself and get sick again.

Being on the Lookout for Warning Signs

In some ways, BSD is like high blood pressure. For most people, high blood pressure doesn't have really noticeable symptoms. You may have a general sense when your blood pressure goes up, but generally there are no specific markers, like a rash or a crippling headache. And yet if you don't take care of it, high blood pressure will make you very sick. It is the leading risk factor for stroke and heart disease.

If you have high blood pressure, you know the best strategy is to take your blood pressure pretty often so you can tell if the treatments are working. You know you should use your knowledge about your blood pressure to adjust your stress load until your blood pressure is under control.

BSD has clear symptoms, including difficulties with your mood, information processing, motivation, and stamina. But they are hard to understand as warning signs of physical changes in your body.

If you don't pay attention to the warning signs of a stress response, you will get sick. These warning signs can include feeling anxious, more irritable, more confused, more elated, or more hypersensitive to noises, people, or situations. This is how your body tells you to slow down and pay attention to your condition. These warning signs are giving you notice to regulate your stress.

And if you regulate your stress, you will break the bipolar cycle—not immediately, not perfectly, but over time. Ava won't have to stay at home after work forever; she just needs to do it for a while as she adapts. And if she does, she will feel in control. With careful monitoring, she will be able to resume many of her old activities. But she has to pace herself.

Dealing with Unavoidable Stress

How can you reduce the impact of major and minor stressors? First, try to make the potentially stressful events and your reactions more predictable. Think about events you are anticipating: changes in your house, your work, your health—even a visit to the dentist. Is there going to be an upcoming family visit? A test at school? A deadline at work? A visit from an annoying friend? A big bill to pay?

What will happen? How will you feel? What skills will be needed to manage that event? How have your abilities to manage the event changed since you got sick?

Is the event very important to you personally—likely to trigger strong feelings? Events will trigger strong feelings if they tap your core values. Can you think about the core values you hold dear? Is achievement very important to you? Is love or nurturing? Or autonomy? Is the situation likely to trigger thoughts about your ability to achieve your core values?

Now try to make the situation a little more controllable. What resources do you have to help you if you have difficulty? The resources might provide technical help or emotional support or anything else you need.

Marie's Story. Let's work through Exercise 13, which is an example of a stressful experience that one patient, Marie, described to us. She was anticipating a holiday visit from her family. As you can see in the chart, the situation was stressful on almost every level. Marie anticipated having to do a lot of shopping and cooking and activity planning, all tasks that require a lot of information processing. She was worried about some of the usual family conflicts that happen when everyone gets together, a situation that might overwhelm her mood-regulation abilities. And it was a situation that was very important to Marie—she couldn't just brush it off. Being with family is a very important part of her life, and it is worth it to her to tolerate this stress. By breaking down the tasks, identifying the stressors, and planning for support, Marie accomplished her goal, without a new episode. If you plan, you will achieve your goals, take risks, and build a meaningful life.

EXERCISE 13
Identifying Stressors

Take a look at the chart Marie completed, and then try to fill out your own version for an upcoming experience that may be stressful for you.

Upcoming Events	How Stressed Do You Feel Thinking About This Event? (rate from 1 to 10) What Are Your Specific Feelings? (e.g., sad, anxious, angry, excited, overwhelmed)	What Are the Information-Processing Demands? (e.g., to think quickly, to remember a lot of information, to learn new things)	What Difficulties Will You Have Regulating Your Mood? (will there be conflict, time pressure, financial pressure?)	Is This Event About Something Important to You Personally—About a Core Value? (e.g., achievement, caretaking, love, independence, health and safety, community, respect, equality, justice)	Coping Strategies—What Can You Do to Make It Easier? (e.g., rest, ask for help, take your time)
Visit from my parents and my sisters	Stress = 8 I am anxious that they won't have fun or that they will make too many demands on me. I am worried that they will be upset when they see me so sick.	Information-processing load = high I will have to plan activities and menus and organize meals.	Mood-regulation difficulties = 6 My mother and my sisters can get into fights. I may be worried about this. I will have to spend money on activities and food. I am a little worried about this.	Love, achievement It is really important to have the family together. I want to be able to be a good host. I am worried that if it doesn't go well, I will feel like a total failure.	It may be really stressful, but I can get support from my mom and dad. I will feel better talking things over with them.

Now it's your turn:

Upcoming Events	How Stressed Do You Feel Thinking About This Event? (rate from 1 to 10) What Are Your Specific Feelings? (e.g., sad, anxious, angry, excited, overwhelmed)	What Are the Information-Processing Demands? (e.g., to think quickly, to remember a lot of information, to learn new things)	What Difficulties Will You Have Regulating Your Mood? (will there be conflict, time pressure, financial pressure?)	Is This Event About Something Important to You Personally—About a Core Value? (e.g., achievement, caretaking, love, independence, health and safety, community, respect, equality, justice)	Coping Strategies— What Can You Do to Make It Easier? (e.g., rest, ask for help, take your time)

Creating Structure

One of the most important ways you can learn to buffer stress is to create more structure in your life. When your daily life gets more predictable, your responses to it get more predictable as well. And when you can count on having to do certain things or having certain satisfying experiences, you will be better able to distract yourself from your own distress and bounce back from difficulty. You may be feeling bad. But if you know you have to go to your volunteer work or to a doctor's appointment (and you get yourself to go), the activity may help you shift your attention away from your internal distress.

What do we mean by structure? Structure includes activities that you do consistently each day and (more or less) regular times for eating and sleeping. Your activities may include daily chores, volunteer work, a full- or part-time job, certain telephone calls—any set activities that you use to structure your day. If you have just been very ill, the list of activities may be short. But as you get better, you will gradually add more to the list. And this is a definite sign of progress.

When Angela (remember her from Chapter 6?) first came to see me, she was not able to do much without getting very anxious or fatigued. We could make a list of all her activities for the week in the first few minutes of the session. Now she is so active that we still make lists of important tasks she has to complete, but we wouldn't have the time to write down all the things she is doing.

You can use this last table to keep track of your waking and sleeping times, your meals, and your daily activities. If you log your activities for a period of time, you will see that you are doing more as you recover. And you are getting better at matching your intentions with your actions—doing the things you want to do. (And if you are not, then it's time to talk to your doctor and figure out what additional help you need.)

EXERCISE 14
Keeping Track of Your Activities

Keep track of the times you wake and sleep and eat. Write in your scheduled activities. Indicate if you were able to do these activities. Use one page per day. Use the lists of urgent and other activities that you made in Chapter 10 to help you structure your daily schedule.

Date and Time	Scheduled Activities	Done?
7 A.M.		
8 A.M.		
9 A.M.		
10 A.M.		
11 A.M.		
12 noon		
1 P.M.		
2 P.M.		
3 P.M.		
4 P.M.		
5 P.M.		
6 P.M.		
7 P.M.		
8 P.M.		
9 P.M.		
10 P.M.		
11 P.M.		
12 midnight		

Date and Time	Scheduled Activities	Done?
1 A.M.		
2 A.M.		
3 A.M.		
4 A.M.		
5 A.M.		
6 A.M.		

Conclusion

What's Next?

In this book, we have given you a lot of information and some tools to help you manage BSD. But we don't expect you to memorize all the facts or use all the tools every day. Instead, we hope you will keep the book handy to read more than once—not all of it, but the parts you need as different issues arise.

You can think about this book in different ways. The book can serve as an exercise manual with chapters devoted to different issues and goals. Most exercise manuals have chapters about weight loss, cardiovascular health, upper-body muscle building, and so on. This book has chapters about stabilizing mood, recognizing your symptoms, talking to your doctor, working on your information processing, and developing stress tolerance.

The exercises can help you develop a systematic approach to recovery. Identify those areas you want to work on, and use the tools we have given you. First, make sure you understand your diagnosis, and more important, recognize the relevant symptoms of BSD you have. Think about your treatments, and develop a plan for monitoring their effectiveness. Identify meaningful goals and "task analyze" them, breaking them into achievable steps that lead to success. Practice detecting stressors and finding ways to buffer their impact.

This book can help you build your support team. Find the trusted people in your life who can help you keep track of symptoms, solve problems, and support you as you (and they) become more expert at managing and recovering from this illness. Your team will include not only health-care providers, family, and friends, but also your coworkers and even employers. We can't work with you one-on-one, but if you use the exercises, we will, in a very real sense, be right there with you.

The book can also serve as a conversation starter. You can use it to make it easier and more straightforward to talk to other people about the way you feel. It can help you to introduce a difficult topic or make it easier to ask for help. How? You can bring your exercise sheets when you visit your doctor, or you can use them to guide conversations with friends and family. You can share the case examples with your family and friends to help them understand the way you feel.

The patients who worked on this book with us wanted to make that contribution. They hoped that sharing the stories of their experiences would make it easier for someone else to communicate more effectively with their therapists, employers, friends, and family members.

So we are not the only people reaching out from these pages. This book is the voice of all the patients and families that have taught us about the meaning of life as they work to recover. They have taught us that it is a gift to ask for help, to share the struggle, and to recognize our shared vulnerability and our shared responsibility to care for each other. BSD is tough. But we can get help and help each other. We can be proud of the struggle and proud of our willingness to keep seeking a better life. Proud that we are interested to see what comes next, who we can be, what we might accomplish. And proud that we will not be ashamed—we will be ourselves.

We want to share one more story with you. The story reminds us about what is important and what can be gained when someone with BSD takes the time to learn about the illness and use strategies systematically to manage the illness (rather than be managed by it). This story also reminded us that no one can, nor should, do it alone.

Recently, Diane turned sixty-five and retired. During the course of the year she spent preparing for her retirement, she wrote an essay about her experiences with mental illness and a speech for her retirement party. The themes she expressed in her essay and her speech communicate so much about the history of the treatment for BSD over the last forty years. Diane's story illustrates how much has changed and how those changes have enabled individuals with BSD to expect to lead meaningful lives.

In her essay, Diane wrote about the history of her experiences with mental illness treatment. She needed to get some of the injustices associated with her early treatment experiences off her chest. Diane got sick with severe bipolar disorder about midway through her college career. Suddenly, she could not tolerate being around the other girls in her sorority house. She isolated herself in the basement. Her thoughts were racing; she had intense and disconnected moods. Her actions were putting her safety at risk. Eventually, she had to leave school. After a series of traumatic personal events brought on by the untreated BSD, she was hospitalized for the first of six times.

In those days (this was the 1960s), the treatments for BSD were generally pretty tough and not very effective. The medication choices were very limited, and many physicians did not know how to use these drugs to control symptoms without crippling side effects. Psychotherapeutic treatments were really still in their infancy. Many patients and their families were blamed for their symptoms and tortured themselves trying to determine how their behavior or thoughts or feelings (conscious or unconscious) could make someone so sick. Fathers and mothers fought over tough love versus spoiling their mentally ill kids.

People spent very long periods in the hospital, hoping that things would get better. Diane spent sixteen months in the hospital the first time she was sent there, much of that time in a locked ward. Here is part of her description of the experience of living in the hospital dormitory in 1963:

> Regarding that dormitory—we could go in there for two hours after lunch to take naps (naps were very desired because of the medications we were on) and otherwise only at night. I guess this is traditional for psychiatric facilities, just like the bathroom behavior, where you had to go with a nurse who observed everything (no doors on the stalls). Your toothbrush and any other articles were kept in the cubbyholes against the wall. You were not allowed to have, say, a jar of hand lotion or anything else that would break. I can, as a matter of fact, *understand* this, but it did add to our feeling of degradation.

It isn't perfect now, but it is much, much better. Diane and I work together to identify her symptoms and stressors. We talk regularly to her psychiatrist, who adjusts her medications as her symptoms change. He offers new medications as they become available, and together we weigh the costs and benefits of changes. We work together with her supervisors at work to make reasonable accommodations as needed so that Diane can earn a living and make a contribution. We talk to her husband to check in and get a second opinion on my judgment and to give and get support.

But still Diane sometimes cycles into hypomania and depression. The symptoms are much milder, and the duration of the episodes is much shorter, because we control the situation, but nonetheless, she still has symptoms. She has some information-processing problems when she gets very anxious or depressed. She still feels suicidal occasionally, because the disorder as a whole is stressful.

But none of that is as important as the fact that Diane really does have a meaningful life. She has just retired from a demanding job. She has a long-standing marriage. She is active in her church and growing active in her community, and she has caring and mutual relationships with other people.

Despite everything, Diane was able to flourish and grow and to talk very openly about her disorder. She worked for an enlightened and remarkable employer, whose supervisors were well educated about disability law. So they were able to work with us to make the job work for Diane as well as for them. For example, initially she had to interact with customers and resolve their problems quickly, even when they were furious. The emotional intensity of the customers was very difficult for her to deal with. So we called her bosses and discussed the situation and asked for some reasonable accommodation. Could she work in an area with a little more consistent set of tasks and away from the high-hostility people for a while? Sure, they responded. Diane is a very conscientious and lovely person, and they wanted to keep her on board. So they reassigned her.

Over the years, we requested (and had approved) three accommodations to her work responsibilities. Each time, Diane and I spoke with her supervisors openly and clearly about her specific symptoms and how they were affecting her and how the specific job demands were making things difficult. Each time, with the appropriate documentation, we were able to work out some other types of arrangements. And each time, Diane was able to maintain her employment and grew in her loyalty and commitment to the workplace.

And she made it all the way to retirement. Now she can sit on her porch in the country and watch the birds. She has time to volunteer in church and join the local chapter of National Alliance on

Mental Illness. And she has time to renew relationships with old friends and make new ones.

She is leading this life because she is up front and straightforward about her condition, and she is graceful and open about her occasional need for help. She works as hard as she can when she is well. And she gets help right away to get back on track when she starts to get sick.

Because she has been open about her situation, other people don't feel powerless or frustrated. They don't feel perplexed by what is happening when she gets sick, they don't feel shy about offering help, and they don't wonder whether she is just goofing off when she takes a sick day. They don't have to waste any time speculating on what's wrong with her, and they don't spend a lot of time making up dumb theories about why she does what she does. They know what to do to have the best possible outcome—for the workplace and for Diane.

Her colleagues recognize that it is an honor to be trusted with the information about her condition. Everyone can feel useful (a good feeling). And the bottom line is that the work at her job got done, Diane earned a living (and a pension), and those involved felt respected, trusted, and safe.

When she retired, her friends at work threw her a huge party. Many people came, even those who worked with her back when she first started. And they ate and celebrated. Diane took the opportunity to thank her supervisors but also to tell her story to everyone so that others who come to the workplace with serious mental illness will be even more accepted and the strategies for making all this work will be clear.

And here is what she said:

It's been wonderful to work with all of you as we faced hundreds of customers each day. This has been more than just a job to me. So I'd like to take just a moment to tell you about myself, so you can appreciate how remarkably kind and supportive you have been and how much I appreciate you. I have suffered with schizoaffective and bipolar disorders since I was around ten, but nobody knew anything about such things then—it was 1951. But I still did well in school and in college until 1962, when the mental illness began to take its toll on me. I ended up in a hospital—the first of at least five—and that ended my college career exactly one year from graduation.

From then on I had my ups and downs for thirty years. This included jumping around from job to job, marriage, two kids, divorce, and remarriage. This second marriage has lasted twenty-eight years come July. My husband is here with me and is certainly one of the major members in my hall of fame. Then in 1993 I came here.

And then Diane went on to thank and nominate for her hall of fame each of the many supervisors who worked with us to make reasonable accommodations—changing assignments or work stations or hours to accommodate her shifting symptoms.

She continued:

Without the help and cooperation of all you kind people, I could not have continued to work. I would have had to spend more time hospitalized. I would surely not be standing here today, surrounded by people who care about me. Today I look around and see friends and supervisors and coworkers, all people with whom I enjoyed working, and who are special to me in many ways. Every one of you treated me like a regular, mentally healthy person and, in fact, thus enabled me to actually be one. This is a priceless gift.

Not every workplace or every supervisor will respond with the human kindness and straightforwardness that Diane's workplace showed. You will have to figure out what your rights and responsibilities are in your particular situation. But the bottom line is that things are changing: the treatments, the law, and public attitudes and knowledge. And this means that Diane, despite having a very severe illness, has been able to build a meaningful life. And you can, too. You will have to figure out how open you want to be and how you want to talk about your condition and your needs.

It's worth remembering that you didn't ask for this, and you have no reason to be ashamed. Getting sick is, unfortunately, part of life. It happens to many of us—and it could happen to any of us. We all benefit when we all care for each other. We get to see the person, not just the symptoms. We share their hopes and dreams and talents and ideas and hard work and courage. The courage shown by our patients gives us courage and hope. It really is inspirational.

What's Next?

Now that you have come this far, it's time to think about where you are going next. We have tried to give you some hopeful visions of what you can achieve. But right now, we would like you to think about how you want your life to look one, five, or even twenty years from now.

With that image in mind, you can become more proactive. Rather than only reacting to symptoms and difficulties, you can also plan and choose goals. You can think about how you would like to see yourself managing the BSD in the future. You can envision what you want your life and relationships to look like. And you can keep your focus on achieving meaningful goals, not only on trying to eliminate symptoms.

Your life won't be perfect if you just "cure" BSD. No one's life is perfect. But you can make your life beautiful and meaningful. You can recognize and manage the symptoms so you can shine through—so you can be you.

Exercises

Here, in one place, are all the exercises provided throughout the book. You can make photocopies of these pages so you can take these exercises with you whenever you need them.

EXERCISE 1
Clarifying Your Diagnosis (Chapter 1)

Write down your diagnosis. It will be easier to manage this disorder
if you are straightforward and clear about what the difficulties are.
If you own your condition, you can begin to manage it.

Your bipolar spectrum diagnosis: _____

Other diagnoses: _____

Additional medical conditions: _____

Ask your doctor what the specific symptoms were that led to the
diagnosis of bipolar disorder. Write them here.

Symptoms: _____

_____

_____

_____

EXERCISE 2
Keeping Track of Your Medical History (Chapter 2)

Fill in your diagnostic history and medication history.

Month and Year	Doctor	Diagnosis	Treatments (medications and doses). List dose changes on a different line.	Effects of Treatment (e.g., mood changes, thinking cleared, ability to function at work, ability to get along with others)	Side Effects (e.g., tremors, weight gain, sleeping problems, sedation, agitation)

EXERCISE 3
Recognizing Depressive Symptoms (Chapter 3)

Symptoms Associated with Depression (from the DSM-IV-TR, p. 356) and the Way People Commonly Describe These Experiences	The Way You Experience These Symptoms
"Depressed mood:" feeling sad, blue, numb; feeling as if you have no energy, no life, no juice	
"Markedly diminished interest or pleasure in activities:" feeling as if you have no motivation, nothing interests you, you can't get anything done because you don't feel like it	
"Significant weight loss when not dieting:" no appetite, food doesn't taste right (or significant weight gain)	
"Insomnia or hypersomnia almost every day:" unable to fall asleep or stay asleep; unable to wake up	
"Fatigue or loss of energy:" feeling exhausted all the time	
"Visible psychomotor retardation or agitation:" feeling as if you can't move or it takes so much effort to move; leaden paralysis; or needing to move, feeling as if you can't keep still	
"Feelings of worthlessness or excessive guilt:" all your memories focus on bad things; feeling as if you are bad or a loser; feeling guilty, responsible for too much; feeling as if there is no point to your life, as if you are always missing out	

Symptoms Associated with Depression (from the DSM-IV-TR, p. 356) and the Way People Commonly Describe These Experiences	The Way You Experience These Symptoms
"Diminished concentration or indecisiveness:" feeling as if your thoughts are very slow or your mind is blank; having difficulty concentrating, focusing, paying attention, keeping your mind on your work; having difficulty remembering important things or even small events during the day	
"Recurrent thoughts of death or suicide:" thinking about death, wanting to die, planning to die	

EXERCISE 4
Recognizing Manic Symptoms (Chapter 3)

Symptoms Associated with Mania (from the DSM-IV-TR, p. 362) and the Way People Commonly Describe These Experiences	The Way You Experience These Symptoms
"Elevated, expansive, or irritated mood:" feeling too good, an abrupt change in your mood; full of optimism; or feeling very angry, irritable, impatient, can't wait for people, think they are taking too long to do things	
"Inflated self-esteem or grandiosity:" having too much confidence, not caring what others think even when you should; having really big ideas—about being able to save the world, attract anyone, do anything; wanting much more attention, being more charismatic	
"Decreased need for sleep:" staying up later or waking earlier without feeling tired	
"More talkative than usual or pressure to keep talking:" talking more quickly than usual or talking or thinking repetitively about the same thing, unable to control the pace or content	
"Flight of ideas or subjective experience that thoughts are racing:" words or ideas jumping around in your head, chaining lots of words together because they sound interesting; sounds or jingles running through your mind	
"Increase in goal-directed activity or psycho-motor agitation:" too much energy—a feeling of restlessness, electric excitement; working too much, collecting too many things, traveling too much, going to too many activities	

Symptoms Associated with Mania (from the DSM-IV-TR, p. 362) and the Way People Commonly Describe These Experiences	The Way You Experience These Symptoms
"Distractibility:" changing the topic all the time; unable to concentrate; feeling as if you have to write everything down to remember	
"Excessive involvement in pleasurable activities that have a high potential for painful consequences:" doing things you know you should not do but feeling like you can get away with it; too much eating, drinking, drug use, spending, partying—without a sense that you can or should stop; sexual attraction to everyone or too much intense attraction to certain people; lots of sexual thoughts in your head	
Other Related Symptoms	
Mood lability: feeling as if you cannot control your mood, as if you cry one minute and are happy the next; being very sensitive; being very angry and irritable, always snapping at other people	
Heightened interpersonal sensitivity: being hyperaware of yourself; feeling as if your skin is too thin; continually focused on interpersonal contacts	

EXERCISE 5
Going to the Doctor: Using Symptom
Descriptions to Communicate with Your Doctor (Chapter 3)

Doctor's name: ....

Date of visit: ....

Current medications: ....

Scheduled: Yes   No   Emergency: Yes   No

Who came with you? ....

Signs and Symptoms	How Do You Feel Today?	How Have You Felt in General Since the Last Appointment?
Sleeping (difficulty falling asleep, difficulty staying asleep, waking too early, sleeping too much)		
Appetite (OK, too much, too little, cravings), weight gain		
Fatigue (rate from 1 to 10; note problems in the morning)		
Concentration (rate from 1 to 10; make notes about activities you can/can't do, like reading, paying bills, talking on the phone, performing tasks at work, planning activities)		

Signs and Symptoms	How Do You Feel Today?	How Have You Felt in General Since the Last Appointment?
Anxiety (rate the intensity from 1 to 10; rate the frequency: never, sometimes, often, always; note any specific circumstances)		
Symptoms of depression (write yours in—e.g., sadness, numbness, guilt, hopelessness, repetitive thoughts—and rate them from 1 to 10)		
Symptoms of mania (write yours in—e.g., grandiosity, excess energy, racing thoughts, too much energy, hypersexuality, irritability, risky behavior—and rate them from 1 to 10)		
Other symptoms (e.g., mood changeability/lability, hypersensitivity to other people)		
Thinking about suicide? Thinking about hurting others?		
Side effects (e.g., sedation, weight gain/loss, sexual difficulties, mood feels funny, difficulty thinking or concentrating, rash, other)		

Signs and Symptoms	How Do You Feel Today?	How Have You Felt in General Since the Last Appointment?
Minor stressors (things that happened that were moderately difficult to deal with)		
Major stressors (things that happened that were very difficult to deal with)		
Other questions or concerns:		
New instructions (medication changes or other advice):		

EXERCISE 6
Medication Tracking Sheet (Chapter 5)

Write in 0 for not at all, 1 for a little, and 2 for a lot. (Note: you may feel more comfortable writing in your own words for the symptoms, as you practiced in Chapter 3.)

	Date	Date	Date	Date	Date
Medications					
Symptoms					
Depressed mood					
Loss of interest or pleasure in activities					
Sleep					
Insomnia (difficulty sleeping)					
Hypersomnia (too much sleeping)					
Appetite					
Loss of appetite					
Increase in appetite					
Energy and movement					
Very low energy, fatigued					
Very slow movements					
Restlessness					
Worthlessness, guilt					

Poor concentration or indecisiveness					
Thoughts about harming or killing yourself					
Plans to kill yourself					
Inflated self-esteem or grandiosity					
Decreased need for sleep					
More talkative or pressure to keep talking					
Racing thoughts, flight of ideas					
Distractibility					
Increased activity					
Too much energy					
Lots of activity					
Too much involvement in pleasurable but potentially harmful activities (overspending, drug use, gambling, etc.)					
Desire to be around other people to talk all the time					
Mood lability (mood changes very frequently or is very sensitive)					
Interpersonal hypersensitivity					
Can't stand being around people					
Very critical of yourself when you are with other people					

Keep worrying or thinking about your interactions with other people					
Feeling very anxious or very self-conscious around other people					
Additional symptoms you notice or improvement you experience					
More hopeful					
More comfortable					
Motivation to get things done					

EXERCISE 7
Your Activities: Charting the Effort Required (Chapter 6)

Write in the tasks you need to do on a daily basis and also some other harder things you have been avoiding. See if you can figure out why some tasks get accomplished and others don't.

Tasks You Need to Do	*How Hard Does It Seem to Do the Task? (on a scale of 1 to 10)*	*Does the Task Get Done? (no, a little, mostly, yes)*	*If Not, What Makes It So Hard? (Does it require a lot of concentration? Does it make you anxious? Does it remind you of being sick? Do you need to talk with other people? Is it too big a job to do all at once?)*

EXERCISE 8
Reconsidering Your Thoughts About BSD (Chapter 7)

Write in your worst-case scenario thoughts. Try to include some daily triggers (thoughts you might have while going about your daily routine). These are thoughts that come up when you see the way BSD affects you in your daily life. Then write in some more reasonable alternatives. If you can't think of a more reasonable approach or are having trouble putting your worst fears into words, do this exercise with someone you care about and trust.

Your Worst-Case Scenario Thoughts	More Reasonable Approaches

EXERCISE 9
Identifying Goal-Setting Thoughts (Chapter 8)

See if you can identify the thoughts you are having as you try to set goals for yourself. Think about your ultimate goals. Then think about possible intermediate steps. If you can't reach your ideal goal now, what would be an intermediate goal, an alternative short-term goal? What are your thoughts and feelings about reaching for a mid-point, a less ambitious or glamorous goal? Or taking a longer time to get there?

Your Long-Term Goal	Your Dream Short-Term Goal	An Alternative Short-Term Goal	Your Worst-Case Scenario Thoughts About Setting This Alternative Short-Term Goal	A More Reasonable Way of Thinking

Use the chart to list as many goals as you can. Then talk the goals over with someone else. Think about whether a specific goal is for right now or a goal for a little later.

Your Goals	Is This a Goal for Right Now or for Later (a Short-Term Goal or a Long-Term Goal)?

EXERCISE 10
Mood Lability Chart (Chapter 9)

One of the most difficult aspects of BSD is that your memories of the way you feel and the way you feel about yourself change as your mood changes. So mood lability can change your sense of your own personal history. It can be helpful to keep track of your moods and the ways they affect your feelings about yourself. In this chart you can keep track of the ways your moods change and how they affect your thoughts about yourself and your ability to be with others. If you are already tracking your symptoms on the table for Exercise 6, you can just add a column there for your thoughts. You might want to pick a regularly scheduled day a week when you spend a few minutes tracking the way you feel—for example, every Thursday evening before you watch a particular show on TV. Then you take a minute to note your mood and your thoughts about yourself and your feelings about one person who is close to you.

Date	Your Mood Right Now (e.g., irritable, sad, relaxed, happy, anxious)	Your Thoughts About Yourself	Your Social Activities (times you were with other people and how you felt)

Date	Your Mood Right Now (e.g., irritable, sad, relaxed, happy, anxious)	Your Thoughts About Yourself	Your Social Activities (times you were with other people and how you felt)

EXERCISE 11
Breaking Down a Difficult Task (Chapter 10)

Now pick a task that is difficult for you to do. Break the task down into little steps, each of which is no harder than a 4. Go back and revisit the goals and steps each week. How did you do? Mark the things that you accomplish. Think about the things you still have trouble doing. Decide if you need to break any steps down into smaller pieces.

Activity	Effort Score (on a scale of 1 to 10)	Why Is It Hard?	What Steps Need to Be Taken to Get It Done?	Did It Get Done? (if not, break it down further)

You can also use the same strategies to make a to-do list for the week. Don't overload the list. Try to improve your ability to make your actions meet your intentions. See if you can really do the things on your urgent list. And try to figure out how long each task will take you. This will help you break the cycle, because you will get better able to predict what you can do and what you should expect each week.

Task list for the week of ....

Urgent	Less Urgent but Still Important	If You Can Get to It

EXERCISE 12
Keeping Track of Progress (Chapter 10)

Here is a special worksheet for keeping track of progress making telephone calls.

Your phone call progress for the week of ....

Kinds of Telephone Calls	Do You Make These Kinds of Calls?	How Much Effort Will It Take to Make This Call? (on a scale of 1 to 10)	Is the Conversation Likely to Involve a Conflict—to Become Emotional or Argumentative?	Will You Need to Understand New Information? (yes or no)	Do You Need to Make Decisions?	Did You Make the Calls?
Making an appointment with a familiar doctor						
Calling a friend to hear about how he or she is doing						
Ordering take-out food						
Calling a repair service to get help						
Calling to correct a billing error						

Kinds of Telephone Calls	Do You Make These Kinds of Calls?	How Much Effort Will It Take to Make This Call? (on a scale of 1 to 10)	Is the Conversation Likely to Involve a Conflict—to Become Emotional or Argumentative?	Will You Need to Understand New Information? (yes or no)	Do You Need to Make Decisions?	Did You Make the Calls?
Calling to complain about a mistake						
Calling to make reservations						
Calling to find out information						
Calling a doctor to ask for information or help						
Calling a store, movie theater, or museum to ask a question about hours or schedules						
Calling to solve a problem in the house						

Kinds of Telephone Calls	Do You Make These Kinds of Calls?	How Much Effort Will It Take to Make This Call? (on a scale of 1 to 10)	Is the Conversation Likely to Involve a Conflict—to Become Emotional or Argumentative?	Will You Need to Understand New Information? (yes or no)	Do You Need to Make Decisions?	Did You Make the Calls?
Calling to work things out with a friend or relative after a dispute						
Calling to ask someone to help you						
Add your own types of calls:						

EXERCISE 13
Identifying Stressors (Chapter 11)

Fill in the chart for an upcoming experience that you think may be stressful for you.

Upcoming Events	How Stressed Do You Feel Thinking About This Event? (rate from 1 to 10) What Are Your Specific Feelings? (e.g., sad, anxious, angry, excited, overwhelmed)	What Are the Information-Processing Demands? (e.g., to think quickly, to remember a lot of information, to learn new things)	What Difficulties Will You Have Regulating Your Mood? (will there be conflict, time pressure, financial pressure?)	Is This Event About Something Important to You Personally—About a Core Value? (e.g., achievement, caretaking, love, independence, health and safety, community, respect, equality, justice)	Coping Strategies—What Can You Do to Make It Easier? (e.g., rest, ask for help, take your time)

Upcoming Events	How Stressed Do You Feel Thinking About This Event? (rate from 1 to 10) What Are Your Specific Feelings? (e.g., sad, anxious, angry, excited, overwhelmed)	What Are the Information-Processing Demands? (e.g., to think quickly, to remember a lot of information, to learn new things)	What Difficulties Will You Have Regulating Your Mood? (will there be conflict, time pressure, financial pressure?)	Is This Event About Something Important to You Personally—About a Core Value? (e.g., achievement, caretaking, love, independence, health and safety, community, respect, equality, justice)	Coping Strategies—What Can You Do to Make It Easier? (e.g., rest, ask for help, take your time)

EXERCISE 14
Keeping Track of Your Activities (Chapter 11)

Keep track of the times you wake and sleep and eat. Write in your scheduled activities. Indicate if you were able to do these activities. Use the lists of urgent and other activities that you made in Chapter 10 to help you structure your daily schedule.

Date and Time	Scheduled Activities	Done?
7 A.M.		
8 A.M.		
9 A.M.		
10 A.M.		
11 A.M.		
12 noon		
1 P.M.		
2 P.M.		
3 P.M.		
4 P.M.		
5 P.M.		
6 P.M.		
7 P.M.		
8 P.M.		
9 P.M.		
10 P.M.		
11 P.M.		

Date and Time	Scheduled Activities	Done?
12 midnight		
1 A.M.		
2 A.M.		
3 A.M.		
4 A.M.		
5 A.M.		
6 A.M.		

Resources

Books

Amador, Xavier (2007). *I am not sick, I don't need help: How to help someone with mental illness accept treatment* (2nd ed.). New York: Vida Press.

This book is an excellent guide to the issues involved in gaining insight into your diagnosis and learning to accept the need for comprehensive care.

Phelps, Jim (2006). *Why am I still depressed? Recognizing and managing the ups and downs of bipolar II and soft bipolar disorder.* New York: McGraw-Hill.

A very readable presentation of the issues involved in diagnosing BSD is presented in this book for patients and families. Dr. Phelps also has an informative website that offers detailed information on the neurobiology of bipolar disorder, psycheducation.org.

Websites

National Institutes of Health (nimh.nih.gov)

Up-to-date information on bipolar disorder and links to other websites with reliable information can be found through the National Institutes of Health's website, specifically at nimh.nih .gov/healthinformation/bipolarmenu.cfm. Another helpful website with good downloadable publications on the benefits and side effects associated with medications used to treat BSD and other psychiatric illness can be found at nimh.nih.gov/publicat/ NIMHmedicate.pdf.

National Alliance on Mental Illness (nami.org)

The National Alliance on Mental Illness website has a wide range of information on psychiatric disorders as well as information about advocacy for people with mental illnesses.

Selected References

We have listed sources for the major topics discussed in each of the chapters. This is not a comprehensive list, but it provides a starting point if you wish to understand more or read the original sources. To make it easier to get the big picture of the research in a particular area, we have included review articles (articles that summarize and evaluate a large body of research) whenever possible. The information is organized by the major subheadings in each chapter.

Throughout the book, our thinking has been influenced by the comprehensive and detailed review of the scientific literature on bipolar disorder found in Goodwin, F. K., & Jamison, K. R. (2007). *Manic-depressive illness: Bipolar and recurrent depression* (2nd ed.). New York: Oxford University Press.

Chapter 1

Why Is It So Important to Learn About BSD?

Angst, J., Gamma, A., & Lewisohn, P. (2002). The evolving epidemiology of bipolar disorder. *World Psychiatry, 1*(3), 146–148.

Hantouche, E. G., & Akiskal, H. S. (2005). Toward a definition of cyclothymic behavioral endophenotype: Which traits tap the familial diathesis for bipolar II disorder? *Journal of Affective Disorders, 96*(3), 233–237.

Saggese, J. M. (2006). The role of recurrence and cyclicity in differentiating mood disorder diagnoses. *Primary Psychiatry, 13*(11), 43–48.

Historical Context

Akiskal, H. S. (2003). Validating "hard" and "soft" phenotypes within the bipolar spectrum: Continuity or discontinuity? *Journal of Affective Disorders, 73*, 1–5.

Akiskal, H. S., & Benazzi, F. (2006). The DSM-IV and ICD-10 categories of recurrent (major) depressive and bipolar II disorders: Evidence that they lie on a dimensional spectrum. *Journal of Affective Disorders, 92*(1), 45–54.

Akiskal, H. S., Bourgeois, M. L., Angst, J., Post, R., Moller, H.-J., & Hirschfeld, R. (2000). Re-evaluating the prevalence of and diagnostic composition within the broad clinical spectrum of bipolar disorders. *Journal of Affective Disorders, 59*, S5–S30.

Akiskal, H. S., Hantouche, E. G., Allilaire, J. F., Sechter, D., Bourgeois, M. L., Azorin, J. M., et al. (2003). Validating antidepressant-associated hypomania (bipolar III): A systematic comparison with spontaneous hypomania (bipolar II). *Journal of Affective Disorders, 73*, 65–74.

Judd, L. L., & Akiskal, H. S. (2003). The prevalence and disability of bipolar spectrum disorders in the U.S. population: Re-analysis of the ECA database taking into account subthreshold cases. *Journal of Affective Disorders, 73*(1–2), 123–131.

Kessler, R. C., McGonagle, K. A., Zhao, S., Nelson, C. B., Hughes, M., Eshleman, S., et al. (1994). Lifetime and 12-month prevalence of DSM-III-R psychiatric disorders in the United

States: Results from the National Comorbidity Study. *Archives of General Psychiatry, 51*, 8–19.

Regier, D. A., Meyers, J. M., Kramer, M., Robins, L. N., Blazer, D. G., Hough, R. L., et al. (1984). The NIMH Epidemiologic Catchment Area Program. *Archives of General Psychiatry, 41*, 934–941.

Weissman, M. M., Bland, R. C., Canino, G. J., Faravelli, C., Greenwald, S., Hwu, H. G., et al. (1996). Cross-national epidemiology of major depression and bipolar disorder. *JAMA, 276*(4), 293–299.

What Are the Symptoms?

Akiskal, H. S. (2000). Mood disorders: Clinical features. In B. Sadock & V. A. Sadock (Eds.), *Kaplan and Sadock's comprehensive textbook of psychiatry* (7th ed.). Baltimore: Williams & Wilkins, 1338–1377.

Amador, X. F., & David, A. (Eds.). (2004). *Insight and psychosis: Awareness of illness in schizophrenia and related disorder* (2nd ed.). Oxford: Oxford University Press.

Angst, J., Gamma, A., Benazzi, F., Adjdacic, V., Eich, D., & Rossler, W. (2003). Toward a re-definition of subthreshold bipolarity: Epidemiology and proposed criteria for bipolar-II, minor bipolar disorders and hypomania. *Journal of Affective Disorders, 73*, 133–146.

Benazzi, F. (2001). Is 4 days the minimum duration of hypomania in bipolar II disorder? *European Archives of Psychiatry and Clinical Neuroscience, 251*, 32–34.

Benazzi, F. (2007). Is overactivity the core feature of hypomania in bipolar II disorder? *Psychopathology, 40*(1), 54–60.

Marneros, A. (2001). Origin and development of concepts of bipolar mixed states. *Journal of Affective Disorders, 67*(1–3), 229–240.

BSD Diagnosis

Diagnostic and Statistical Manual of Mental Disorders (*DSM-IV*
Text Revisions) (4th ed.). (2000). Washington, DC: American
Psychiatric Association.

Chapter 2

The Struggle for an Accurate Diagnosis

Angst, J., Sellaro, R., Stassen, H., & Gamma, A. (2005). Diagnostic conversion from depression to bipolar disorders: Results of a long-term prospective study of hospital admissions. *Journal of Affective Disorders, 84*(2–3), 82–91.

Artashez, P., Fargian, S., Levi, A., Yeghiyan, M., Gasparyan, K., Weizman, M., Weizman, A., Fuchs, C., & Poyurovsky, M. (2006). Obsessive-compulsive disorder in bipolar disorder patients with first manic episode. *Journal of Affective Disorders, 94*, 151–156.

Benazzi, F. (2006). Impact of temperamental mood lability on depressive mixed state. *Psychopathology, 39*(1), 19–24.

Goldstein, B. I., Velyvis, V. P., & Parikh, S. V. (2006). The association between moderate alcohol use and illness severity in bipolar disorder: A preliminary report. *Journal of Clinical Psychiatry, 67*, 102–106.

Judd, L. L., Akiskal, H. S., Schettler, P. J., Coryell, W., Maser, J., Rice, J. A., Solomon, D. A., & Keller, M. B. (2003). The comparative clinical phenotype and long-term longitudinal episode course of bipolar I and II: A clinical spectrum or distinct disorders? *Journal of Affective Disorders, 73*, 19–32.

Judd, L. L., Akiskal, H. S., Schettler, P. J., Endicott, J., Maser, J., Solomon, D. A., et al. (2003). A prospective naturalistic investigation of the long-term weekly symptomatic status of bipolar II disorder. *Archives of General Psychiatry, 60,* 261–269.

Judd, L. L., Akiskal, H. S., Schettler, P. J., Endicott, J., Maser, J., Solomon, D. A., Leon, A. C., Rice, J. A., & Keller, M. B. (2002). The long-term natural history of the weekly symptomatic status of bipolar I disorder. *Archives of General Psychiatry, 59*(6), 530–537.

Luty, S. E., Joyce, P. R., Mulder, R. T., Sullivan, P. F., & McKenzie, J. M. (2002). The interpersonal sensitivity measure in depression: Associations with temperament and character. *Journal of Affective Disorders, 70,* 307–312.

Matza, L. S., Rajagopalan, K. S., Thompson, C. L., & de Lissovoy, G. (2005). Misdiagnosed patients with bipolar disorder: Comorbidities, treatment patterns and direct treatment costs. *Journal of Clinical Psychiatry, 66*(11), 1432–1440.

McIntyre, R., Soczynska, J. K., Bottas, A., Bordbar, K., Konarski, J., & Kennedy, S. (2006). Anxiety disorders and bipolar: A review. *Bipolar Disorders, 8*(6), 665–676.

Sato, T., Bottlender, R., Kleindienst, N., & Moller, H. J. (2005). Irritable psychomotor elation in depressed inpatients: A factor validation of mixed depression. *Journal of Affective Disorders, 84,* 187–196.

Simon, N. M., Otto, M. W., Fischmann, D., Racette, S., Nierenberg, A. A., Pollack, M. H., & Smoller, J. W. (2005). Panic disorder and bipolar disorder: Anxiety sensitivity as a potential mediator of panic during manic states. *Journal of Affective Disorders, 87,* 101–105.

Srakowski, S. M., DelBello, M. P., Fleck, D. E., & Arndt, S. (2000). The impact of substance abuse on the course of bipolar disorder. *Biological Psychiatry, 48,* 477–485.

Chapter 3

Living in the Bipolar Cycle

Carver, C. S., & Scheier, M. F. (1998). *On the self-regulation of behavior.* Cambridge, England: Cambridge University Press.

Dailey, G. (2007). Assessing glycemic control with self monitoring of blood glucose and HgA1c measurement. *Mayo Clinic Proceedings, 82,* 229–236.

Ghaemi, S. N., Sachs, G. S., Chiou, A. M., Pandurangi, A. K., & Goodwin, K. (1999). Is bipolar disorder still underdiagnosed? Are antidepressants overutilized? *Journal of Affective Disorders, 52*(1), 135–144.

"Is It Me or BSD?"

Akiskal, K., Akiskal, H. S., Allilaire, J. F., Azorin, J. M., Bourgeois, M. L., Sechter, D., et. al. (2005). Validating affective temperaments in their subaffective and socially positive attributes: Psychometric, clinical and familial data from a French national study. *Journal of Affective Disorders, 85*(1–2), 29–36.

Perugi, G., & Akiskal, H. S. (2002). The soft bipolar spectrum redefined: Focus on the cyclothymic anxious-sensitive, impulse-dyscontrol, and binge-eating connection in bipolar II and related conditions. *Psychiatric Clinics of North America, 25*(4), 712–737.

Valenca, A. M., Nardi, A. E., Nascimento, I., Lopes, F. L., Freire, R. C., Mezzaslma, M. A., Veras, A. B., & Versiani, M. (2005). Do social anxiety disorder patients belong to a bipolar spectrum subgroup? *Journal of Affective Disorders, 86,* 11–18.

Looking at the Complete Picture

Aksikal, H. S. (2005). Searching for behavioral indicators of bipolar II in patients presenting with major depressive episodes: The "red sign," the "rule of three" and other biographic signs of temperamental extravagance, activation and hypomania. *Journal of Affective Disorders, 84*(2–3), 279–290.

Akiskal, H. S., Hantouche, E. G., & Lancrenon, S. (2003). Bipolar II with and without cyclothymic temperament: "Dark" and "sunny" expressions of soft bipolarity. *Journal of Affective Disorders, 73*(1–2), 49–57.

Pirozzi, M. M., Magliano, L., Fiorillo, A., & Bartoli, L. (2006). Agitated "unipolar" major depression: Prevalence, phenomenology, and outcome. *Journal of Clinical Psychiatry, 67*(5), 712–719.

Stafstrom, C. E., Rostasy, K., & Minster, A. (2002). The usefulness of children's drawings in the diagnosis of headaches. *Pediatrics, 109*(3), 460–472.

Chapter 4

Why It's Good to Know

Miklowitz, D. J., George, E. L., Richards, J. A., Simoneau, T. L., & Suddath, R. L. (2003). A randomized study of family-focused psychoeducation and pharmacotherapy in the outpatient management of bipolar disorder. *Archives of General Psychiatry, 60*, 904–912.

A System of Connections

Manji, H. K., & Lenox, R. H. (2000). The nature of bipolar disorder. *Journal of Clinical Psychiatry, 61*(suppl. 13), 42–57.

Phillips, M. L. (2006). Neural basis of mood dysregulation in bipolar disorder. *Cognitive Neuropsychiatry, 11*(3), 233–245.

The Overall Structure of the Nervous System

Baddeley, A. (2003). Working memory: Looking back and looking forward. *Nature Reviews Neuroscience, 4*, 829–839.

Bear, M., Connors, B., & Paradiso, M. (2007). *Neuroscience: Exploring the brain*. Baltimore: Lippincott, Williams, and Wilkinson.

Ellenbogen, M. A., Hodgins, S., Walker, C. D., Courture, S. A., & Adam, S. (2006). Daytime cortisol and stress reactivity in the offspring of parents with bipolar disorder. *Psychoneuroendocrinology, 31*, 1164–1180.

Funahashi, S. (2006). Prefrontal cortex and working memory. *Neuroscience, 139*(1), 251–261.

Gross, J. J. (1998). The emerging field of emotion regulation: An integrative review. *Review of General Psychology, 2*(3), 271–299.

Lupien, S. J., Fiocco, A., Wan, N., Maheu, F., Lord, C., Schramek, T., & Tu, M. T. (2005). Stress hormones and human memory function across the lifespan. *Psychoneuroendocrinology, 30*, 225–242.

Respovs, G., & Baddeley, A. (2006). The multicomponent model of working memory: Explorations in experimental cognitive psychology. *Neuroscience, 139*(1), 5–21.

Richards, J. M., & Gross, J. J. (2000). Emotion regulation and memory: The cognitive costs of keeping one's cool. *Journal of Personality and Social Psychology, 79*(3), 410–424.

Yildiz-Yesiloglu, A., & Ankerst, D. P. (2006). Neurochemical alterations of the brain in bipolar disorder and their implications for pathophysiology: A systematic review of the in-vivo proton magnetic resonance spectroscopy findings. *Progress in Neuro-Psychopharmacology and Biological Psychiatry, 30*(6), 969–995.

How Cells in the Brain Communicate

Catapano, L. A., & Manji, H. K. (2007). G protein coupled receptors in major psychiatric disorders. *Biochimica Et Biophysica Acta, 1768*(4), 976–993.

Einat, H., & Manji, H. K. (2005). Cellular plasticity cascades: Genes-to-behavior pathways in animal models of bipolar disorder. *Biological Psychiatry, 59*, 1160–1171.

Green, E., & Craddock, N. (2003). Brain-derived neurotrophic factor as a potential risk locus for bipolar disorder: Evidence, limitations, and implications. *Current Psychiatry Reports, 5*(6), 469–476.

Your Brain and Other Symptoms of BSD

McClung, C. A. (2007). Circadian genes, rhythms and the biology of mood disorders. *Pharmacology and Therapeutics, 114*(2), 222–232.

Ozcan, M. E., & Banoglu, R. (2003). Gonadal hormones in schizophrenia and mood disorders. *European Archives of Psychiatry and Clinical Neuroscience, 253*(4), 193–196.

Neurobiology and Your Medications

Bear, M., Connors, B., & Paradiso, M. (2007). *Neuroscience: Exploring the brain.* Baltimore: Lippincott, Williams, and Wilkinson.

Schatzberg, A. F., & Nemeroff, C. B. (Eds.). (2001). *Essentials of clinical psychopharmacology.* Washington, DC: American Psychiatric Publishing, Inc.

Chapter 5

"Can't I Just Pop a Few Pills?"

Emilien, G., Septien, L., Brisard, C., Corruble, E., & Bourin, M. (2007). How far are we from a rigorous definition and effective management? *Progress in Neuro-Psychopharmacology and Biological Psychiatry, 31*, 975–996.

Newman, C. F., Leahy, R. L., Beck, A. T., Reilly-Harrington, N. A., Gyulai, L., Newman, C. F., et al. (2002). *Pharmacotherapy in the context of cognitive therapy for patients with bipolar disorder.* Washington, DC: American Psychological Association.

The Role of Medications in BSD

Gitlin, C., Swendsen, J., Heller, T. L., & Hammen, C. (1995). Relapse and impairment in bipolar disorder. *American Journal of Psychiatry, 152*, 1635–1640.

Mitchell, P. B., Malhi, G. S., Redwood, B. L., & Ball, J. (2003). Summary of guidelines for the treatment of bipolar disorder. *Australasian Psychiatry, 11*(1), 39–53.

Stankowski, J., Friedman, S. H., & Sajatovic, M. (2006). A review of the guidelines for drug treatments for bipolar disorder. *Current Medical Literature: Psychiatry, 17*(1), 1–6.

Yatham, L. N., Kennedy, S. H., O'Donovan, C., Parikh, S. V., MacQueen, G., McIntyre, R. S., et al. (2005). Canadian Network for Mood and Anxiety Treatments (CANMAT) guidelines for the management of patients with bipolar disorder: Consensus and controversies. *Bipolar Disorders, 7*, 5–69.

Yatham, L. N., Kennedy, S. H., O'Donovan, C., Parikh, S. V., MacQueen, G., McIntyre, R. S., et al. (2006). Canadian Network for Mood and Anxiety Treatments (CANMAT) guidelines for the management of patients with bipolar disorder: Update 2007. *Bipolar Disorders, 8*(6), 721–739.

"Which Medication Is for Me?"

Cousins, D. A., & Young, A. H. (2007). The armamentarium of treatments for bipolar disorder: A review of the literature. *International Journal of Neuropsychopharmacology, 10*(3), 411–431.

Ellingrod, V. L., Bishop, J. R., Moline, J., Lin, Y.-C., & Miller, D. D. (2007). Leptin and leptin receptor gene polymorphisms and increases in body mass index (BMI) from olanzapine treatment in persons with schizophrenia. *Psychopharmacology Bulletin, 40*(1), 57–62.

Keating, G. M., & Robinson, D. M. (2007). Quetiapine: A review of its use in the treatment of bipolar disorder. *Drugs, 67*(7), 1077–1095.

McIntyre, R. S., Mancini, D. A., Basile, V. S., Srinivasan, J., & Kennedy, S. H. (2003). Antipsychotic-induced weight gain: Bipolar disorder and leptin. *Journal of Clinical Psychopharmacology, 23*(4), 323–327.

Sachs, G. S., Nierenberg, A. A., Calabrese, J. R., Marangell, L. B., Wisniewski, S. R., & Gyulai, L., et. al. (2007). Effectiveness of adjunctive antidepressant treatment for bipolar depression. *New England Journal of Medicine, 356*(17), 1711–1722.

Shaltiel, G., Dalton, E. C., Belmaker, R. H., Harwood, A. J., & Agam, G. (2007). Specificity of mood stabilizer action on neuronal growth. *Bipolar Disorders, 9*(3), 281–289.

Smith, L. A., Corneilius, V., Nornock, A., Bell, A., & Young, A. H. (2007). Effectiveness of mood stabilizers and antipsychotics in the maintenance phase of bipolar disorder: A systematic review of randomized controlled trials. *Bipolar Disorders, 9*(4), 394–412.

Voruganti, L. P., & Awad, G. A. (2004). Is neuroleptic dysphoria a variant of drug-induced extra-pyramidal side effects? *Canadian Journal of Psychiatry, 49*(5), 285–289.

Describing Your Symptoms

Brondolo, E., & Mas, F. (2001). Cognitive-behavioral strategies for improving medication adherence in patients with bipolar disorder. *Cognitive and Behavioral Practice, 8*(2), 137–147.

Roy, H. P. (2007). Use of treatment guidelines in clinical decision making in bipolar disorder: A pilot survey of clinicians. *Current Medical Research & Opinion, 23*(3), 467–475.

What About Your Treatment?

Harrington, J., Noble, L. M., & Newman, S. P. (2004). Improving patients' communication with doctors: A systematic review of intervention studies. *Patient Education & Counseling, 52*(1), 7.

Pendleton, D., Schofield, T., Tate, P., & Havelock, P. (2003). *The new consultation: Developing doctor-patient communication.* Oxford: Oxford University Press.

Roter, D. L., & Hall, J. A. (2006). *Doctors talking with patients/ patients talking with doctors: Improving communication in medical visits.* Westport, CT: Auburn House.

Practical Considerations

McAlpine, D. D., & Mechanic, D. (2000). Utilization of specialty mental health care among persons with severe mental illness: The role of demographics, need, insurance, and risk. *Health Services Research, 35*(1–2), 277–292.

Sturm, R., & Wells, K. (2000). Health insurance may be improving, but not for individuals with mental illness. *Health Services Research, 35*(1–2), 253–262.

Chapter 6

Lack of Motivation

Akiskal, H. S. (2005). The dark side of bipolarity: Detecting bipolar depression in its pleomorphic expressions. *Journal of Affective Disorders, 84*(2–3), 107–115.

Akiskal, H. S., & Benazzi, F. (2005). Atypical depression: A variant of bipolar II or a bridge between unipolar and bipolar II? *Journal of Affective Disorders, 84*(2–3), 209–217.

Bauer, M. S., Altshuler, L., Evans, D. R., Beresford, T., Williford, W. O., & Hauger, R. (2005). Prevalence and distinct correlates of anxiety, substance, and combined comorbidity in a multi-site public sector sample with bipolar disorder. *Journal of Affective Disorders, 85*(3), 301–315.

Baumeister, R. F., & Vohs, K. D. (2007). Self-regulation, ego depletion, and motivation. *Social and Personality Psychology Compass, 1*, doi: 10.1111/j.1751-9004.2007.00001.X

Gollwitzer, P. M., & Bargh, J. A. (1996). *The psychology of action: Linking cognition and motivation to behavior.* New York: Guilford Press.

Knutson, B., & Cooper, J. C. (2005). Functional magnetic resonance imaging of reward predictions. *Current Opinions in Neurology, 18*, 411–417.

McClure, S. M. (2004). The neural substrates of reward processing in humans. *Neuroscience, 10*, 260–268.

Salamone, J. D., Correa, M., Farrar, A., & Mingote, S. M. (2007). Effort-related function of nucleus accumbens dopamine and associated forebrain circuits. *Psychopharmacology, 191*(3), 461–480.

The Desire to Try

Muraven, M., & Baumeister, R. F. (2000). Self-regulation and depletion of limited resources. Does self-control resemble a muscle? *Psychological Bulletin, 126*(2), 247–259.

Emotion and Physical Pain

McEwen, B. (2007). Physiology and neurobiology of stress and adaptation: Central role of the brain. *Physiological Reviews, 87*(3), 873–904.

Miller, A. H., & Manji, H. K. (2006). On redefining the role of the immune system in psychiatric disease. *Biological Psychiatry, 60*(8), 796–798.

Von Korff, M., & Simon, G. (1996). The relationship between pain and depression. *British Journal of Psychiatry, Supplement, 30,* 101–108.

Why You Really Don't Feel Like It

Carver, C. S., & Scheier, M. F. (2002). Control processes and self-organization as complementary principles underlying behavior. *Personality and Social Psychology Review, 6*(4), 304–315.

Chapter 7

"How Could This Happen to Me?"

Bazner, E., Bromer, P., Hammelstein, P., & Meyer, T. D. (2006). Current and former depression and their relationship to the effects of social comparison processes: Results of an Internet-based study. *Journal of Affective Disorders, 93*(1–3), 97–103.

Gruman, J. (2007). *Aftershock: What to do when the doctor gives you—or someone you love—a devastating diagnosis.* New York: Walker & Company.

Triggers in Everyday Life

Beck, J. (1995). *Cognitive therapy: Basics and beyond.* New York: Guilford Press.

Ellis, A. (2001). *Overcoming destructive beliefs, feelings and behaviors: New directions for Rational Emotive Behavior Therapy.* New York: Prometheus Books.

Depression and the Desire to Recover

Pettit, J. W., & Joiner, T. E. (2006). *Chronic depression: Interpersonal sources, therapeutic solutions.* Washington, DC: American Psychological Association.

Chapter 8

Setting Realistic Goals

Bauer, M. S., & McBride, L. (2003). *Structured group psychotherapy for bipolar disorder: The Life Goals Program* (2nd ed.). New York: Springer Publishing Co.

Social Comparisons

Ellis, A. (1977). Using Rational Emotive Therapy techniques to cope with disability. *Professional Psychology Research and Practice, 28*(1), 17–22.

Guimond, S. (Ed.). (2006). *Social comparison and social psychology: Understanding cognition, intergroup relations, and culture.* Cambridge: Cambridge University Press.

Uchino, B. N., Cacioppo, J. T., Kiecolt-Glaser, J. K. (1996). The relationship between social support and physiological processes: A review with emphasis on underlying mechanics and implications for health. *Psychological Bulletin, 119,* 448–531.

Not-So-Realistic Goals

Amador X. F., Andreasen N. C., Flaum M., Strauss D. H., Yale S. A., Clark S., & Gorman, J. M. (1994). Awareness of illness in schizophrenia, schizoaffective and mood disorders. *Archives of General Psychiatry, 51*(10), 826–836.

Amador X. F., Strauss D. H., Yale S., Gorman J. M., & Endicott, J. (1993). Assessment of insight in psychosis. *American Journal of Psychiatry, 150*(6), 873–879.

Elgie, R., & Morselli, R. L. (2007). Social functioning in bipolar patients: The perception and perspective of patients, relatives and advocacy organizations. *Bipolar Disorder, 9*(1–2), 144–157.

Yen, C. F., Chen, C. S., Ko, C. H., Yen, J. Y., & Huang, C. F. (2007). Changes in insight among patients with bipolar I disorder: A 2-year prospective study. *Bipolar Disorders, 9*(3), 238–242.

Chapter 9

Mood-Regulation Problems

Gross, J. J. (2007). *Handbook of emotion regulation.* New York: Guilford Press.

Johnson, S. L., Sandrow, D., Meyer, B., Winters, R., Miller, I., Solomon, D., & Keitner, G. (2000). Increases in manic symptoms following life events involving goal attainment. *Journal of Abnormal Psychology, 109*, 721–727.

Phillips, M., Drevets, W. R., Rauch, S. L., & Lane, R. (2003). Neurobiology of emotional perception I. *Biological Psychiatry, 54*(5), 504–514.

Getting Stuck In Your Thoughts and Moods

Thayer, J., & Lane, R. D. (2002). Perseverative thinking and health: Neurovisceral concomitants. *Psychology and Health, 17*(5), 685–695.

Behavioral Strategies

Maczka, G., Siwek, M., Dudek, D., & Grabski, B. (2005). Bipolar disorder—from a biological to an integrative approach: The role of cognitive-behavioral therapy in the treatment of bipolar disorder. *Archives of Psychiatry and Psychotherapy, 7*(3), 37–45.

Chapter 10

"Why Don't I Feel as Smart as I Used To?"

Bearden, C. E., Glahn, D. C., Monkul, E. S., Barrett, J., Najt, P., Kaur, S., Sanches, M., Villarreal, V., Bowden, C., & Soares, J. C. (2006). Sources of declarative memory impairment in bipolar disorder: Mnemonic processes and clinical features. *Journal of Psychiatric Research, 40,* 47–58.

Benabarre, A., Vieta, E., Martinez-Aran, A., Garcia-Garcia, M., Martin, F., Lomena, F., Torrent, C., Sanchez-Moreno, J., Colom, F., Reinares, M., Brugue, E., & Valdes, M. (2005). Neuropsychological disturbances and cerebral blood flow in bipolar disorder. *Australian and New Zealand Journal of Psychiatry, 39,* 227–234.

Clark, L., Sarna, A., & Goodwin, G. M. (2005). Impairment of executive function but not memory in first-degree relatives of patients with bipolar I disorder and in euthymic patients with unipolar depression. *The American Journal of Psychiatry, 162*(10), 1980.

Doyle, A. E., Wilens, T. E., Kwon, A., Seidmen, L. J., Faraone, S. V., Fried, R., Swezey, A., Snyder, L., & Biederman, J. (2005). Neuropsychological functioning in youth with bipolar disorder. *Biological Psychiatry, 58,* 540–548.

Nehra, R., Chakrabarti, S., Pradhan, B. K., & Khehra, N. (2006). Comparison of cognitive functions between first- and multi-episode bipolar affective disorders. *Journal of Affective Disorders, 93*, 185–192.

Pavuluri, M. N., Schenkel, L. S., Aryal, S., Harral, E. M., Hill, E. M., Herbener, E. S., & Sweeney, J. A. (2006). Neurocognitive function in unmedicated manic and medicated euthymic pediatric bipolar patients. *American Journal of Psychiatry, 163*, 286–293.

Robinson, L. J., Thompson, J. M., Gallagher, P., Goswami, U., Young, A. H., Ferrier, I. N., & Moore, P. B. (2006). A meta-analysis of cognitive deficits in euthymic patients with bipolar disorder. *Journal of Affective Disorders, 93*, 105–115.

Rybakowski, J. K., Borkowska, A., Skibinska, M., Szczepankiewicz, A., Kapelski, P., Leszczynska-Rodziewicz, A., Czerski, P. M., & Hauser, J. (2005). Prefrontal cognition in schizophrenia and bipolar illness in relation to Val66Met polymorphism of the brain-derived neurotrophic factor gene. *Psychiatry and Clinical Neurosciences, 60*, 70–76.

Breaking Down the Problem and Building Up Your Supports

Bellack, A. S., Gold, J. M., & Buchanan, R. W. (1999). Cognitive rehabilitation for schizophrenia: Problems, prospects, and strategies. *Schizophrenia Bulletin, 25(2)*, 257–274.

Von Korff, M., Gruman, J., Schaefer, J., Curry, S. J., & Wagner, E. H. (1997). Collaborative management of chronic illness. *Annals of Internal Medicine, 127*, 1097–1102.

Working Memory and Interpersonal Relationships

Mart'nez-Arán, A., Vieta, E., & Colom, F. (2004). Cognitive impairment in euthymic bipolar patients: Implications for clinical and functional outcome. *Bipolar Disorders, 6*(3), 224–232.

Reeder, C., Newton, N., Frangou, S., & Wykes, T. (2004). Which executive skills should we target to affect social functioning and symptom change? A study of a cognitive remediation therapy program. *Schizophrenia Bulletin, 30*(1), 87–100.

Keeping Track of Successes

Scheier, M. F., & Carver, C. S. (2005). Effects of optimism on psychological and physical well-being: Theoretical overview and empirical update. *Cognitive Therapy and Research, 16*(2), 201–228.

Chapter 11

Seasons and Weather

Lee, H-C., Tsai, S-Y., & Lin, H-C. (2007). Seasonal variations in bipolar disorder admissions and the association with climate: A population-based study. *Journal of Affective Disorders, 97*(1–3), 61–69.

Stress

Altman, S., Haeri, S., Cohen, L. J., Aleksey, T., Barron, E., & Galynker, I. I., et. al. (2006). Predictors of relapse in bipolar disorder: A review. *Journal of Psychiatric Practice, 12*(5), 269–282.

Brondolo, E. (1998). Affirming core values: A cognitive approach for use in the treatment of anger and anxiety problems. *The Behavior Therapist, 21*, 57–87.

Kauer-Sant'Anna, M., Tramontina, J., Andreazza, A., Cereser, K., Costa, S., Santin, A., Yatham, L., & Kapczinski, F. (2007). Traumatic life events in bipolar disorder: Impact on BDNF levels and psychopathology. *Bipolar Disorders, 9,* 128–135.

Lazarus, R. S. (1991). *Emotion and adaptation.* New York: Oxford University Press, Inc.

Lazarus, R. S., & Folkman, S. (1984). *Stress, appraisal, and coping.* New York: Springer.

Pearlin, L. I. (1989). The sociological study of stress. *Journal of Health and Social Behavior, 30,* 241–256.

Creating Structure

Craighead, W. E., Miklowitz, D. J., Frank, E., Vajk, F. C., Nathan, P. E., & Gorman, J. M. (2002). *Psychosocial treatments for bipolar disorder.* New York: Oxford University Press.

Frank, E., Kupfer, D. J., Thase, M. E., Mallinger, A. G., Swartz, H. A., Eagiolini, A. M., et al. (2005). Two-year outcomes for interpersonal and social rhythm therapy in individuals with bipolar I disorder. *Archives of General Psychiatry, 62*(9), 996–1004.

Zaretsky, A. E., Rieve, S., & Parikh, S. V. (2007). How well do psychosocial interventions work in Bipolar Disorder? *Canadian Journal of Psychiatry, 52*(1), 14–21.

Additional References

Throughout this book, our suggestions reflect standard cognitive behavioral techniques used to treat a variety of health conditions. Specifically, we use basic behavioral skills, including task analysis or applied behavioral analysis, to break down the day-to-day difficulties experienced by people with BSD. We also use many techniques from cognitive therapy, incorporating the work of Albert Ellis and Aaron Beck.

In addition, much of the overall approach is based on behavioral medicine interventions for chronic medical diseases including diabetes or hypertension. These approaches are based on the understanding of the psychological and biological effects of stress on health. Some aspects of these approaches are also consistent with the ideas of Social Rhythm Therapy.

The ideas in this book overlap with many of the ideas presented in the references that follow, but they do not represent all the different kinds of psychosocial interventions that have been validated for the treatment of bipolar disorder. It may be useful for you to learn more about empirically validated treatments for BSD. We have listed some books written for clinicians that describe psychosocial treatment approaches to BSD. You may find it helpful to ask your doctors to discuss the approaches presented in these books with you.

Basco, M. R., McDonald, N., Merlock, M., Rush, A. J., & Wright, J. H. (2004). *A cognitive-behavioral approach to treatment of bipolar I disorder.* Washington, DC: American Psychiatric Publishing, Inc.

Frank, E., Swartz, H. A., Johnson, S. L., & Leahy, R. L. (2004). *Interpersonal and Social Rhythm Therapy.* New York: Guilford Press.

Johnson, S. L., & Leahy, R. L. (2004). *Psychological treatment of bipolar disorder.* New York: Guilford Press.

Miklowitz, D. J., Akiskal, H. S., & Tohen, M. (2006). *Psychosocial interventions in bipolar disorders: Rationale and effectiveness.* Hoboken, NJ: John Wiley & Sons Inc.

Newman, C. F., Leahy, R. L., Beck, A. T., Reilly-Harrington, N. A., & Gyulai, L. (2002). *Bipolar disorder: A cognitive therapy approach.* Washington, DC: American Psychological Association.

Otto, M. W., Reilly-Harrington, N., Hofmann, S. G., & Tompson, M. C. (2002). *Cognitive-behavioral therapy for the management of bipolar disorder.* New York: Guilford Press.

Ramirez Basco, M., & Rush, A. J. (2005). *Cognitive-behavioral therapy for bipolar disorders* (2nd ed.). New York: Guilford Publications.

Scott, J., & Leahy, R. L. (2004). *Cognitive therapy of bipolar disorder.* New York: Guilford Press.

Swartz, H. A., Markowitz, J. C., Frank, E., Hofmann, S. G., & Tompson, M. C. (2002). *Interpersonal psychotherapy for unipolar and bipolar disorders.* New York: Guilford Press.

Index